DELIVER US FROM EVIL

Restoring the Soul in a

Disintegrating Culture

RAVI ZACHARIAS

WORD PUBLISHING

NASHVILLE LONDON VANCOUVER MELBOURNE

WORD PUBLISHING

Unless otherwise indicated, Scripture quotations used in
this book are from the Holy Bible, New International Version (NIV).
Copyright © 1973, 1978, 1984 International Bible Society. Used by
permission of Zondervan Bible Publishers.

Excerpts from Peggy Noonan's essay, "You'd Cry Too If It
Happened to You," in chapter 10 are reprinted by permission
of *FORBES* magazine © Forbes Inc., 1992.

Book design by Mark McGarry
Set in Caslon & Caslon Antique

Library of Congress Cataloging-in-Publication Data
Zacharias, Ravi K.
Deliver us from evil / Ravi Zacharias.
p.   cm.
Includes bibliographical references.
ISBN 0-8499-1395-0 (HARDCOVER)
ISBN 0-8499-3950-X (TRADE PAPER)
1. Christianity and culture—History—20th century.
2. Moral conditions. 3. Apologetics. I. Title.
BR115.C8Z33   1997
270.18'2—dc20   96-34666
CIP

Printed in the United States of America

0 1 2 3 4   QWM   9 8 7 6 5 4 3 2

To Sarah, Naomi, and Nathan,
whose lives have been enriched by
many cultures,
but whose hearts belong to God.

The ideas that shaped our culture were great and worthy. The principal goal was to reconcile liberty with law. But in the last century our culture has undergone incredible changes and challenged the ideas that once shaped and guided us. The result has been the collapse of law, the eradication of the spirit, and the unleashing of evil.

The response of the Christian calling for a return to morality is a scream in the dark, because morality has no self-sustaining light. It is a vacuous term left at the mercy of our passions.

Only in the defense and authority of the Word can morality be anchored, evil understood, and the soul restored.

Contents

vii

Foreword

PICTURE THIS:

A vast, teeming sea of people stretching as far as the eye can see, boiling, agitated. Most are wearing Walkman headsets and the latest fashions; every person has the most recent issue of *USA Today* in one hand and a television remote control in the other. Some are quite educated, but still lost. Some are lost, but don't care. All are shouting, chanting, bumping into each other as each tries to march in his own direction, spouting a favorite truism. There is no right or wrong, so no one feels ashamed; all opinions are equal, so no one is allowed to think; religious convictions are private, so they are meaningless in any discussion. It's like a massive tabloid talk show gone berserk.

But there is one figure out there that isn't moving, like a reef standing dry above the crashing surf. The man is dark-skinned and gentle-eyed with a crown of white hair, and he is speaking firmly, steadily, in measured tones to whomever will listen. It's easy to pass him by: he has no traveling band, no loud PA system, no stage smoke or lights, no premium giveaways or easy goodies from God.

All he has is wisdom—the kind you have to sit still to receive; the kind you must take in small bites and chew slowly.

But if you truly wish to know, he'll tell you how this unruly mob got this way, and suggest the way to find peace and direction again.

He'll even show you where the solid rocks are in this ocean so you can stand steady above the tossing waves.

I happen to appreciate his boldly standing there, giving his lectures, writing his books, teaching, debating, getting bumped and jostled like the rest of us but standing steady nevertheless. The media don't provide disclaimers, the politicians don't come with subtitles, opposing opinions don't list their ingredients on the package. But he's been digging into these things for years and he's ready to help us do the same.

People often ask me where I get my ideas and what books I read. Well, I read novels to learn from the styles and techniques of other fiction writers, but to gain wisdom and insight into our times, I turn often to those who have already hacked a trail through the jungle of ideas: people like C.S. Lewis, Francis Schaeffer, Josh McDowell, and someone I've just recently discovered, Ravi Zacharias.

In *Deliver Us from Evil* this brilliant thinker writes on a subject that has been the primary theme of my novels: the mystery of evil. Though he was hard at work on his calling long before I even started mine, and though he paints with a different brush stroke, many of you already know about him and his work. For the newcomers like myself, I can only say welcome and congratulations on your find. The Bible says "a gray head is found in the way of wisdom," and I can affirm that his hair is far whiter than mine.

Frank E. Peretti

Acknowledgments

WINSTON CHURCHILL described the writing of a book in metaphors ranging from "a monster" to "a master." While those images attend as deadlines stare one in the face, a book is more than anything else the documentation of a thought life on a specific subject. In that sense an author alone knows how much he or she is indebted to others. To list all whose writings and ideas I have interacted with is impossible. But those whose immediate effort has made the transference from thought to script possible are more readily and easily acknowledged. They too are many.

I would like to thank my research assistant, Danielle DuRant, for being a determined and dedicated "seeker of sources." She has helped me track down numerous thoughts once read but in need of retrieval. My assistant, Nancy Bevers, is always able and willing to pull loose ends together as the project nears completion. The staff at Word Incorporated are a writer's delight. They do their end of the work with excellence and contagious courtesy. Kip Jordon and Joey Paul are dear friends. They have interacted with the material with heart and mind, beyond the call of duty. The editorial help from Jan Dennis and Sue Ann Jones is immensely valued, as is the project management by Laura Kendall. I must also mention that throughout this writing my colleagues led by Dan Glaze have been my best friends. They have encouraged me beyond measure and prayed that this book will meet a very specific need in a society so clearly at risk. So many others have stood alongside them to help keep me going.

Finally and most importantly my debt in this book is to my wife, Margie. If there is anyone else whose heart is interwoven with concern for content and effect as passionately as mine, it is hers. I thank her for the hours of work and patience. But neither of us could have afforded the time needed if it had not been sacrificially given to us by our three children. This book is rightfully dedicated to them.

All that is good in here reflects that which comes from the Author of Life. All that falls short is from yours truly.

Ravi K. Zacharias
Atlanta, 1996

Introduction:
Vandalized by Wickedness

IF THERE IS an image that mirrors the mind of the West today, it is strikingly reflected in Oscar Wilde's *The Picture of Dorian Gray*. This familiar story describes an exceptionally handsome young man so physically captivating that he drew the persistent and awe-stricken adulation of a great artist. The artist talked him into being the subject of a portrait, saying he had never seen a face more attractive and pure. When the painting was completed and presented to young Dorian he became so fixated and enraptured by his own looks that he wistfully expressed the longing to draw license from such beauty and to live any way he pleased, unfettered by any restraint. Any ensuing disfigurement from a dissolute life he hoped would mar only the picture, leaving him unblemished.

Like Faust of old, Dorian received his wish. His life of sensuality, indulgence, and even murder left his physical appearance completely untainted. Spurred on by the success of his undiscovered duplicity, he plummeted ever further into the depths of wickedness. One day, alone and pensive, he uncovered the portrait he had kept hidden for all those years, only to be numbed by the hideousness of the face, which bore the horror and scars of a life scandalously lived.

Besieged by the fear of being found out and of the incriminations the portrait would reveal, he buried it among the goods he kept stowed in his attic. But the pathetic charade came to an end one day when the artist himself laid eyes on it. Overcome with grief because of what he knew it meant, he confronted Dorian and implored him to turn his wasteful life around and seek God's forgiveness. "Does it not say somewhere," he pled, "'Come now let us reason together. Though your sins be as scarlet, they shall be as white as snow. Though they be red like crimson, they shall be as white as wool'?" In a fit of rage Dorian Gray grabbed a knife and killed the artist, silencing the voice.

The story reaches an emotional climax when, no longer able to stand the indictment of the picture, Dorian reached for the knife once more to destroy the portrait and remove the only visible reminder of his wicked life. The moment he thrust the blade into the canvas the portrait returned to its pristine beauty, and Dorian Gray himself lay stabbed to death on the floor. The ravages that had marred the picture now so disfigured his own countenance that he was unrecognizable to the servants who heard the scream of death and came rushing in to help.

The power of this book lies in its most central idea: [Can an individual or a society live with complete disregard for a moral and spiritual center and not suffer from the wounds of wickedness? Can the soul of a people who have lived without restraint be left unravaged? Is there a point at which one must cry a halt to the passions and the whims of unbridled appetite and admit that enough is enough?] Ironically, Oscar Wilde himself is renowned for his disdain of any moralizing. It was he who said that "form is content," "nothing succeeds like excess," and "nothing is good or bad, only charming or dull." He died at the age of forty-six, finding out that it was easier to live out his maverick philosophy in art than in life.

The book has a grave message for the West, so imbued with strength, so splendidly attractive, and so rich in resources. But here, too, the culture is living with philosophical risk, not pausing to uncover, even for a moment, the ramifications for the soul. One strongly suspects that in story after story that headline the news almost every day of the week there is betokened a deep disfigurement in the soul of a culture. Tragedies and atrocities are common fare, and in any corner coffee shop discussions can be heard of the latest horror or carnage to strike at our communities. Evil has taken on forms and concoctions that shock the world. Any catalog at the end of any given year tells a painful story of what is happening in our streets and homes and institutions.

But it will not do to just bemoan the reality or to condemn the evil. Much more is required of us as thinking people before we can get past the symptoms and diagnose how this has all come about. Behind an act is a thought or a belief, and those thoughts unleashed in anti-social behavior make the headlines. Yet seldom are these thoughts and beliefs scrutinized. When that is done we, like Oscar Wilde, may find out that though we may play with sinister ideas in our imaginations and artistic escapes, we cannot do the same with life. The ideas we now popularly espouse are reshaping our culture, redefining our destiny, and are at the heart of the rampant evil that we now witness. They are ideas, therefore, that must be seriously questioned or we will find ourselves in some remorse-filled future, wondering how it all happened. It is in order to thwart such a possibility—and even more to guard the soul from the vandalizing attacks of seemingly innocent ideas in our culture—that this book is written.

As we journey through the thinking that has shaped the present, we will highlight the shifts we have made along the way and the losses we have incurred. Losses that, if left unaddressed, cannot but make life unlivable. How did these losses come about? How, for example, does America today make decisions on the deepest questions of life if there is no single vision or consensus of spirit? The intent of this analysis is to wrestle with these questions as they have surfaced and affected not just America but all of the West. Here we will understand the real nature of a culture in the midst of a revolution, a culture plagued with what we now call the mystery of wickedness.

I have divided the material in this book into three sections, the first of which I have titled "The Moods of the Present." In this section the ideas and circumstances that spawned our present cultural struggle are underscored. The postmodern mind and contemporary passions are rigorously examined in the light of the moods they have engendered with such cultural force. Secular social theories bring with them inescapable entailments that are logically connected to the ideas themselves. If the idea is believed and lived out, the outcome is inevitable. A few decades ago Francis Schaeffer described our culture as one that had its feet planted firmly in midair. Things have changed since then. Our feet are now firmly planted on a field of ideas mined with explosive theories that have been proven to be devastating. Even uncertainty is preferable to wrongheaded confidence.

This first section of the book is the most difficult because of necessity it deals with the thinking in the formative stage of Western consciousness. This section will focus particularly upon the secular concepts that helped frame the present. We will delve into the traits that left their mark upon the birth of a nation. But as remote as some of the influences may seem at first, the argument is critical to our understanding. To borrow from the Dorian Gray analogy again, there was no single act that has led to the present disfigurement. The process was gradual as choices were made because of philosophies espoused. Gaining an understanding of our cultural journey will enable us to see how far we have come and how far off we have ended from where we first began. As theoretical and philosophical as these issues may seem, they are vitally important. Once this material is covered, we will break free to the inspirational and more engaging thrust of the subject. The answers can then be measured against this backdrop.

In the second section we will hear from "The Voices of the Past." These are voices that can be heard from across the centuries, voices of religious import that have conditioned Western culture possibly more than any others. There is an attempt today to silence some of these voices, but they too must be heard. "Those who cannot remember the past," said George Santayana, "are condemned to repeat it."[1] We will see from these first two sections that philosophy and religion have had their day. Tragically, in the hands of society's powerbrokers, both often exploited people, and neither could stem the tide of evil. For decades social theorists trumpeted the glories of the Renaissance and the Enlightenment. They made great boasts that those historic movements would be the salvation of mankind. Today that optimism has been blunted, and that anticipation has left admitted disappointment. If anything, postmodernism has mocked the promise once offered by modernity and called its bluff. But an even greater contempt is felt by some toward the voice of religion as it informs either education or law and particularly as it addresses morality. Here the disconcerting reality stands in clear view. History tells a sorry tale of the dismal failure of politicized religion and even of the masses who used and abused it to their own impoverishment. Evil was still at center stage. There are at once some sobering and actually thrilling lessons here. We must give ear to these truths.

Finally, we will examine the options available to us as a whole generation lives in the silence of apprehension and fears "The Face of the Future." To the subtle yet real forces that influence and even control our culture, there must be given due recognition and response. In an unprecedented fashion, events and atrocities are now confronting us with disorienting impact. With increasing frequency journal articles and scholarly writings voice the bedeviling question of unmitigated evil and cry for answers. Here we find the common ground of what threatens all of us. And from that common ground the answers will become clear and possibly inescapable. In the light of the past and the moods of the present we can help shape the face of the future. The potency of the answers calls for a response of the heart, mind, and soul and cannot be ignored. Neutrality on these issues is impossible.

A final note of caution as we begin: The focus of this study may seem to be on one particular nation, America, but do not be misled. The struggles addressed and the truths uncovered here apply not only to America but to the entire West and indeed, to our whole world. Whether one likes it or not, America today is, if not the quintessential embodiment of the Western rationalist tradition, certainly on the cutting edge of that mind-set and shares in the soul of postmodern Western civilization. Yet despite the aberrations that exist in her cultural conflict, there is also in her spirit a belief in the reasonableness of deliberation and a yearning for answers that address the soul. Therefore, though we are focusing on this one nation, let it be clear that the implications and applications of the truths are global. Even the so-called nonsecular and religiously dominated cultures of the world had better pay due heed to the truths we will uncover.

With wise choices, as we reason together there is the real possibility that a nation so great and a culture so generous—one that has given much to the world—can contend for good and be restored in her soul, and that her countenance may reveal a spiritual beauty of essence and not merely of style. Such restoration always begins with individuals, and such is my hope and prayer as these thoughts are penned.

Part 1

The Moods of the Present

One

The Winds of Change

THERE IS AN ancient Eastern parable instructively titled "The Wealth Is Nearer to You Than You Think." It tells of a wealthy merchant who had undertaken a lengthy journey, carrying with him his most valuable jewels. Along the way, another traveler befriended him, making it look like a chance meeting but with the sole intent of laying his hands on those precious stones. At the end of each day when they arrived at a local inn they would share the room for the night. As was customary, each received his mat and pillow and also a wash basin with a towel for his nightly ablutions.

The merchant, somewhat suspicious of his newfound friend's real motives, devised a scheme to safeguard his valuables that was to leave his ill-intentioned companion completely befuddled. Before they turned in for the night, he would graciously offer the would-be thief the privilege of washing up first. As soon as the thief would leave the room, the rich man would take his bag full of precious stones and hastily hide it under the pillow of the thief. When the thief would return, the rich man would make his exit, taking his turn at cleaning

Ablutions — cleansing w/ water or liquid as rel. ritual

up. Awaiting this moment of opportunity, with predatorial glee the rogue would plunge into the rich man's belongings, rummaging through his bag, even ransacking in and under the rich man's pillow, feverishly searching for the precious stones. His frenzied and fruitless attempts at every stop left him utterly frustrated, and eventually he would lay his sleepless head on his pillow, angry at his failure to locate the treasure.

Finally, as it came time to part on their last day together, the rich man began his farewell pleasantries and, to the speechless astonishment of his companion, informed him that all along he had been painfully aware of his real motives. Then came the agony-inflicting revelation: "You poured all your energies into looking everywhere—except under your own pillow. The wealth was nearer to you than you realized."

This story, with all the markings of country wisdom, has a clear injunction that stirs the Eastern imagination by weaving a simple truth about life into a profound proverbial climax. But it is a parable with a wealth of wisdom to offer to the West as well, which appears at this time in its own cultural journey to be in search of an all-embracing value by which it can define itself. Surrounded by vociferous and confident secular theories on life's purpose and destiny, and becoming increasingly aware of radically different world-views from its own, there is a restlessness within and a frenetic search for some new idea that will assuage its impoverished spirit.

If a consortium of thinkers were to gather and give serious thought as to what defines the West in its primary pursuit, it would be impossible to find a consensus. At best, one might cynically observe that the essence of Western culture is its willingness to die for a higher standard of living. But that would be unfair, because in the midst of the ideational war the gnawing recognition that consistently emerges from social critics is that all is *not* well and that the world's malady has very little to do with any economic solutions. In such diagnoses is the concession that material gains alone have not quenched the deep-seated hunger of the soul, a hunger we share with all humanity.

AN UNFULFILLED SPIRIT IN A
MATERIALISTIC CULTURE

This sense that something is missing spiritually is exacerbated by the tacit admission that in and through our harried lives the culture in which we find ourselves is in turmoil. Among the elderly, a sense of fear overwhelmingly dominates their outlook while the young unblushingly confess to a sense of emptiness within. Those in their middle years often capture these twin agonies with a veiled apprehensiveness that bespeaks an uncertainty in an increasingly hostile world. But when one probes deeper into these felt realities what stands out is the lack of a clear cultural scaffolding on which to build one's values, or a distinctive identity from which a cultural ethos may be drawn. Culture has become like a dress code, varying with the time of the day and presence or absence of the elite. Such drastic variables have blurred the lines of demarcation within which we may navigate our lives.

In spiritual terms the only statement one can confidently make is that the West is engaged in a momentous battle, one in which it is risking its very soul.[1] No, it may not be as overt or as consciously sinister as Goethe's *Faust* or Wilde's *Dorian Gray*. But let us make no mistake about it: The ramifications are the same when the destiny of the soul is traded for the enthrallment of the moment. With the increasing awareness in the West of other cultures and religions, there is honest doubt about the adequacy of traditional answers on matters of the spirit, and many now believe we must instead search under "other cultural pillows" to find the real treasure.

Ironically, the search for a "soul-fulfilling idea" looms uppermost at the end of the greatest century of human progress, a century in which the West has decidedly played the lead. This irrepressible pursuit cannot easily be cast aside even though some in academia may wish it were possible. For although such terms as *progress* and *wealth* are common in the Western socioeconomic lexicon, the reality is that millions of people, though blessed by material abundance and dynamic options in life, still seek liberation from their personal enslavement to habits and from pursuits that have brought disintegration within and fragmentation without.

While we prowl and scavenge relentlessly through a variety of lifestyles in search of that all-fulfilling treasure, we seem to have forgotten that this hyperactive pursuit and empty-hearted feeling are not new to the human experience. The Bible, through the prophet Haggai, called upon the people of his day to take note of their indulgences, which were also attended by diminishing returns:

> Give careful thought to your ways. You have planted much, but have harvested little. You eat, but never have enough. You drink, but never have your fill. You put on clothes, but are not warm. You earn wages, only to put them in a purse with holes in it. (Hag. 1:5–6)

AN UNEASY AMERICA IN A NERVOUS WORLD

As old as the malady is, this existential bewilderment of the West has caught many by surprise because it has come at the end of this much heralded century of humanism's zenith. As knowledge in every field grew exponentially, the assumption was made that the loftiest dreams of the human spirit would finally be attained. Instead, those hopes have been dashed, and the answers that were sought after have become more remote than ever. Though the intellect has conquered new ground, the will is still plagued by old weaknesses, and the mind is incapable of either explaining the spirit's hungers or of taming the heart's passions. Honest seekers of truth have begun to feel as if they

lexicon - vocab. of particular language, field, social class, person - dictionary are being trampled underfoot from all directions, and they are having to buckle and stretch like artificial turf upon which intellectual games are being played out.

The world bears the scars of numerous wars and carries the grief of horrendous crimes committed at the whims of demagogues who stormed into history and bloodied it in the process. Political and social theories that were touted as advances for society begat criminal experiments that were justified by the promise of utopia but left in their wake the slaughter of millions. The cost exacted in human suffering has staggered the imagination. At the midpoint of this century, the sobering effects of the human frailty that brought about these global tragedies left political leadership around the world painfully aware of a crisis of the spirit. For a while, a concerted commitment was made to right the wrongs that lost sight of human worth and to bind humanity once again for the common good. The West began to do some serious soul-searching, and the years of rebuilding a broken world began, with America at the forefront.

But suddenly and turbulently in the decade of the 1960s a self-mutilating cultural upheaval burst upon the American scene that cut to the very core of the nation's soul. She was now engaged in a war of her own, searching for an identity by which she might define herself and a cultural soil from which she could sprout anew. The world was watching. Every standard of right and wrong was up for redefinition. For America nothing compares with the fallout this upheaval has brought.

What two world wars did to rudely awaken the world in general from its own apathetic slumber, the 1960s did to America, enshrouding her in a tense cultural struggle that has not yet left the national consciousness. The fires of internal conflict that burned within the hearts of the student world at that time, stoked by the fuel of a losing war effort, generated a cloud of cynicism that the winds of political change have not dissipated.

A NEW DIRECTION FOR AN OLD REBELLION

With haunting and ubiquitous force, the mood of that decade has resurfaced, laying claim to the nation itself. The death of Jerry Garcia of the Grateful Dead rock group prodded many of his followers to note that the spirit of the sixties is very much alive. This time-lapse effect sustained a long-held maxim that the books read and the philosophies imbibed in one's teens and twenties erupt with a delayed effect, exerting redoubled influence in one's middle years.

For America this has proven to be undeniably true. The Vietnam War came to an end and the Paris Peace Treaty was concluded, yet something vastly more important remained unresolved—the moral conflict that raged as radical ideas and social theories refashioned a culture. At that time many believed that this revolution could be contained because it was merely the student world—a subsection of the culture—that was in revolt against the system. One could draw some consolation from the security that at least theoretically there was a system, an establishment, that could deal with the revolt and stem the tide.

That was a costly miscalculation. We are presently witnessing a more radical agenda built upon the revolutionary zeal of three decades ago. Now, however, it is no longer students rebelling against the system; it is the system itself that is in revolt against the very ideas on which it was built. Listen to the haughty pronouncement of this long-awaited upheaval in the words of Middlebury College English professor Jay Parini:

> After the Vietnam War, a lot of us [antiwar graduate students] didn't just crawl back into our library cubicles; we stepped into academic positions. With the war over, our visibility was lost, and it seemed for awhile—to the unobservant—that we had disappeared. Now we have tenure, and the work of reshaping the universities has begun in earnest.[2]

Ubiquitous - omnipresent

AN APATHETIC POSTURE TO AN
AGGRESSIVE CULTURE

One leading academic has described this as a revolution from the top down. As bastions of intellectual strength have taken the lead, the conflict has come into the mainstream of culture with even deadlier force and now occupies center stage in our cultural struggle. The clash within the American mind in search of an identity is insightfully discussed by authors such as Dinesh D'Souza[3] in *Illiberal Education* and Myron Magnet[4] in *The Dream and the Nightmare*. But one wonders whether the popular mind is paying any heed to the troubling signs to which these authors are pointing. The old story about a student who was asked whether ignorance or apathy was worse and answered, "I don't know, and I don't care," is not humorous to anyone who knows the stakes in such a conflict.

There are terrifying analogies in the history of geopolitical conflict that speak to this common indifference to the reshaping power of society's gatekeepers. When Karl Marx, for example, was buried at London's Highgate Cemetery, only eleven people attended his graveside funeral. In his eulogy Friedrich Engels was more prophetic than the world then conceded when he spoke of the enduring potency of Marx's ideas. Who at that time would have believed what Marx's thought and philosophy would exact from our world? Who would have by the wildest stretch of imagination thought of a Mao Zedong or a Joseph Stalin who would harness that philosophy and plunder the soul of a people? Now, in the cultural revolt that is under way in America, the same apathy prevails. The assumption is made that the changes taking place are those of a people coming of age. The dire reality of a nation whose soul is endangered and whose youth live on the knife edge of irrational definitions of life is unaddressed.

Yet the proponents of this revolution have spoken of their vision. There is a clear call to uproot the sentinels of decency that line the past and to reconfigure the future without any points of reference. Magnet reminds us of this in his reference to Norman Mailer's prediction in the 1950s of "a new kind of man" who would enter the arena of ideational conflict:

Concept

> He was the hipster, who knew from the atom bomb and the Nazi concentration camps that societies and states were murderers, and that under the shadow of mass annihilation one should learn . . . to give up "the sophisticated inhibitions of civilization," to live in the moment, to follow the body and not the mind, "to divorce oneself from society," and "to follow the rebellious imperative of the self," to forget "the single mate, the solid family, and the respectable love life," to choose a life of "Saturday night kicks," especially orgasm and marijuana. For 1957, this was prophetic. It contained in a nutshell much of the self-liberation part of the cultural program of the sixties.[5]

For those who thought that the frisking and frolicking Gadarene herd of sinister ideas from the sixties had been drowned in the sea of the past, it is terribly daunting to hear of their sevenfold return to a house not properly cleansed. But there is incontrovertible reason for this, and it must be addressed.

The primary question has been raised: Has the West forged a new self-consciousness and disfigured its soul as a result? Has there been a wanton squandering, or forfeiture, of its spiritual wealth? Forfeiture, I say, because it is precisely that—the casting aside of what was once the source of our national life and the pervading influence in all relations and institutions. In this resulting maelstrom of conflicting ideas one may legitimately ask why this revolt has come about, against whom it has come, how it has come to be, and whether it is possible for us as a culture to find a stable road ahead. The issues are of supreme importance and must be addressed if we are to understand why our culture is at risk and how serious the implications are for every household and life.

Maelstrom - powerful, hazardous whirlpool state of affairs, tumultuous

A MAP FOR THE MIND IN THE MAZE
OF A CONFLICT

Thankfully there are answers and there is hope. To glibly sing the words from "America the Beautiful"—"Thine alabaster cities gleam undimmed by human tears"—is only to mock the hurts and torments of families living with brokenness and fear in our troubled cities, cities that merely reflect the larger hurt the nation is experiencing. But the unfolding lyrics—"Confirm thy soul in self-control, thy liberty in law"[6]—cause the emotions to swell with hope that the eyes of grief may be unblurred and that we might once again see our cities throb with the happy laughter of children unafraid.

It is time for us to reason together, because the issues are immense. But let us be absolutely sure that *reason* is not the same as *intellect*, or the brain. As the brain informs the body, the mind informs the soul. The distinction is important. And it is the mind that needs to be addressed if the soul is to be saved. The mind, unlike the brain, does not feed on isolated and fragmentary bits of information. It frames its response to both the intellectual and the existential challenge of knowing and living.

This whole controversy of the human mind transcending the human brain is not incidentally or accidentally at the forefront of academic debate today. That very quest reveals how deep the search for identity has gone. Ironically, this discussion recently intensified when the world's chess champion, Gary Kasparov, narrowly escaped defeat by a computer. With no humor intended, Kasparov said he had undertaken the computer challenge to preserve the dignity of humanity. If the world champion escaped defeat by the skin of his chess prowess, one must wonder what that would have said for us if an ordinary person had been mercilessly humiliated by the thinking machine.

But there is the clue. The computer does not feel mercy when inflicting loss or feel wonderful when enjoying the triumph of its victory. Information and data do not make a person. As humans, many senses coalesce in our daily lives. The mind-set by which we live blends together more than academic megabytes. The hurts and loves, the fears and aches, the dreams and nightmares we experience condition the way we look at reality. We speak of the wholeness of our beings because we cannot live with the absurdity of being reduced to sheer matter. The mind blends the values of our convictions with the thoughts of reality, and we respond with purpose and feeling. We are more than programmed chess players. We do not want to be pawns risked in ideational warfare. The glory of human experience transcends a game and defies scientific dissection. That glory lies in humanity's "soulishness." The cultural revolt that was spawned in educated minds proved that the brain can be well fed while the spirit is starved and that people are more than ideas.

The old adage still speaks: The world was made for the body, the body was made for the soul, and the soul was made for God. When that discovery is made and the soul is restored in a disfigured culture, we find the greatest treasure of all—and it is nearer to us than we realize.

Two

Dying Beliefs and Stillborn Hopes

TRUTH IS STRANGER than fiction, it is said, but as G. K. Chesterton has appropriately declared, that may well be because we have made fiction to suit ourselves. There is possibly a more disturbing reason for our estrangement from truth, particularly if that truth signifies a reality that is terrifying and unchangeable. Our inability to alter what is actual frustrates our grandiose delusions of being sovereign over everything. And that may be at the heart of why we find truth to be so strange. Remorse offers no relief to one seeking an escape from an irreversible situation. Any hope that the nightmarish present is just a dream or that it is erasable by merely wishing the opposite dissipates in the face of a stern, concrete reality.

Some years ago a friend shared just such a heartrending story—the truth of which seemed much stranger than fiction. To do full justice to the poignancy of the incident I must briefly describe the surroundings that occasioned my being privy to it. We were sitting in the parking lot of a historic building, a venue for gatherings of the gatekeepers of society. An air of sophistication surrounded all who entered. I was preoccupied with an address I was to deliver on the problem of the emptiness that stalks our younger generation, growing up in a time of such moral confusion. The arrival of a rather prominent individual prompted my host, a minister, to recount his story in very somber tones.

"There goes our federal prosecutor," he said, "a fine man I met under very tragic circumstances." As he labored through the details of their first contact, I knew this was not just another crisis in a minister's routine but an ineradicable scar on his pastoral heart.

He told me of a young couple he had married some years ago who had represented to him every ideal worth emulating. They embodied excellence to the youth of the church. Both were preparing to practice medicine and were on sizable merit scholarships. As he had driven away in his car after performing their wedding ceremony, my host had rehearsed in his mind the grand occasion it had been; in all his years of ministry he had not seen a more radiant couple. He thrilled at the prospect of all that lay ahead of them.

But then, like a shattered dream, only a few months into the marriage came a dreadful awakening. In the predawn hours of a wintry night the pastor's telephone rang, and a distraught voice begged him to come. The caller, the young man of such promise, kept stuttering the words, "I think I've killed her! I think I've killed her!" The minister hastily dressed and rushed over to the couple's home only to find the young woman lying lifeless in her bed and the young husband sobbing inconsolably at her side.

What had happened? What had brought about this tragedy? After a long time of prying and pleading, the story was finally uncovered. Some weeks earlier this young woman had discovered that she was pregnant. With years of study still ahead, neither of them wanted to start a family so soon. This sudden turn of events unsettled all their plans, driving them desperately in search of a solution. They considered every option. Finally, words escaped her lips that she had never dreamed she would utter. "This is completely devastating," she said. "There is no other way but to abort this child if our careers are to survive."

The very suggestion opened a deep rift between them. They were both known on their campus for their outspoken conviction of the sanctity of the child's life in the womb. They fervently believed that each unborn child had a right all its own. Now, circumstances beyond their control had invaded their absolutes; "fate" had threatened their autonomy. Conviction clashed with ambition, and they agonized over a private decision they hoped would never be betrayed in public.

That is when she proposed her final solution. "Let's do this at home," she said. "You bring all the equipment we need to the apartment, and no one need ever know." As a young medical student, he felt this could be accomplished, and so they nervously laid meticulous plans for that fateful night. The young man was not yet fully trained in the administration of an anesthetic, and as he stumbled through the procedure he unwittingly gave her a much larger dose than he should have. His greatest fear became a ghastly deed, and he lost her. In the panicky moments that followed, with trembling hands and a cry of desperation he reached for the telephone and uttered those remorse-ridden words, "Pastor, please hurry and come to our apartment. I think I've killed her!"

ENCOMPASSED BY POSSIBILITIES

Anyone who has experienced the consequences of an act which no amount of human ingenuity can undo knows the horror of such a feeling. The most painful aspect of such a feeling is that it is a stark reminder of our finitude, which before the unchangeable consequence had thought itself omnipotent. It is not my intention to use this experience to validate one side or the other of the abortion debate. I only share it because in this nightmarish event, every individual and societal struggle that we as a civilization now face seems crystallized, and our institutions seem powerless to find a solution. For here, deeply held convictions collided at cross-purposes with career goals. Here, church and state met with equal dismay and sorrow. Here, private solutions sought escape from public castigation. Here, technology goaded a mind into a high-risk decision. Here, expediency compromised wisdom. And here, human sovereignty lay crushed by its own hands. In short, the confrontation between religious belief and a preferred lifestyle left a bloody trail.

This incident dramatically demonstrates that the moral options we face are more confounding than ever as technology, education, and cultural shifts have become powerful factors in our decision-making. At the same time we are all aware that the dilemmas we will increasingly face will not be restricted to the controversial matters of abortion or sexuality; nor will they be in the uncharted terrain of genetic engineering or euthanasia, nor, for that matter, even in the vastness of global issues such as violence, ethnic cleansing, or AIDS. Inexorably, our search for ever-increasing prosperity carries with it unprecedented entailments and costs as new technologies developed apart from moral considerations become available. These are undoubtedly monumental concerns, life-altering in their scope. But as divisive as they are, these issues are only the "above-ground" manifestations of a deep foundational shift in our culture, whose proud boast is self-determination and whose legitimizing license provides the very basis for our decision-making. If that foundation, which continues to shift under many strains, settles unevenly, the once stable infrastructure standing upon it will be imperiled, and a total collapse is only a matter of time.

Of one thing we can be certain: The range of our choices in life will be on the rise. Life has begun to resemble a smorgasbord where the entrees are laid before us in an alluring array, making us ever more gluttonous but with proportionately diminishing satisfaction. The cycle of imbibing and disgorging that characterizes gluttony is not just physical; it ultimately cuts deeply into the very spirit of our human experience. And if recognized too late, the symptoms of the bulimic spirit could destroy our very souls.

We must understand, therefore, that it is not just the range of choices that must bear study; the greatest scrutiny must be paid to *how* and *why* we make our individual and societal decisions. As a rule we are each prone to giving due attention to the specific decisions that confront us individually every day. We are also mindful of how those decisions bring about change. But the decisions are commonly based on reasons that themselves are not thought through. When those reasons are examined, they often prove to be unblushingly spurious and would result in chaos if everyone operated by the same principles. The implications of our choices carry over into what we call *lifestyles*. Individually they may seem to be insignificant, but when the mind-set of a whole culture is altered in accordance with those choices, the ramifications are staggering.

History is replete with examples of unscrutinized cultural trends that were uncritically accepted yet brought about dramatic changes of national import. Social analysts recognize that there has never been a time like our present, when such bold-faced positions are espoused and such carriers of change prevail. It is not sufficient to say, "This is just the way it is," when the intellectually curious demand the rationale for why it must be so. The appropriate response to Bertrand Russell's explanation of the universe—"It's just there"—is to remind him that the question is not one of the existence or nonexistence of the universe but of the "why" of its existence. And even more to the point, why do we even ask why it is there? The same applies to every culture. Our practices cannot be dismissed with a "just there" attitude. Cultures have a purpose, and in the whirlwind of possibilities that confront society, reason dictates that we find justification for the way we think and why we think, beyond chance existence.

ENDANGERED BY PROXIMITY

influence of culture

Few influences in life are as dominant—and as faltering—as the power of culture. There is implicitly in all of us a tacit surrender to its demands while we supposedly boast individuality and freedom of thought. That subtle entrapment by itself ought to alert us to the ambiguity of privilege and peril in being part of a drifting culture that carries us unaware into turbulent waters. This subsuming effect of culture is analogous to the heartbeat of a people. Let me illustrate how all-absorbing culture can be.

A medical doctor who is a friend of mine suffered a serious heart attack while still in his thirties. He described the pain of that event as different from any other pain he had ever felt. He had always experienced every prior injury or hurt, whether a broken arm or a sore knee, as a hurt to a part of his body. In some measure he could separate himself from the pain. "But during my heart attack," he said, "I was *in* the pain. There is no other way to describe it." The notion conveyed is instructive—that the very organ that should have been pumping life was instead disseminating pain.

I can think of no better analogy to describe the all-consuming hold of culture as it becomes the source of thinking and feeling in its members. So engulfing is this power that we cannot discuss the essential theme of our culture at its crossroads without being locked into it ourselves. We are *in* it, and we are hard pressed to find a fulcrum outside of it with which to leverage a shift.

IMPERILED BY IMMERSION

An old Chinese proverb says if you want to know what water is don't ask the fish. The fish does not know any other kind of life because it is submerged in the monotony and single vision of a watery existence. To the fish, no other existence is possible; hence, it can conceive of nothing by which to measure its own existence.

fulcrum - support or point of rest on which a lever turns in a moving body.

Similarly, it is important for those immersed in a culture to recognize that proximity does not necessarily guarantee an accurate perspective. Sometimes a culture can so imperceptibly absorb and transmit ideas into its consciousness that it is hard for those within it to be objective about the propriety of its practices when measured against a counter-perspective. In other words, if we want to know what America is like, the surest way to gain that understanding may not be to ask one who has been culturally American all his or her life.

Admitting this blind spot is not easy, though it plagues us all and breeds a subtle form of prejudice. I well recall my own struggle with cultural awareness in the early days of my relocation from one part of the world to another. I would become very agitated whenever I heard public speakers report on their impressions of recent trips they had taken to the land of my birth, because they often came back with reports of shocking and heartrending conditions. This troubled me greatly for it seemed exaggerated, embellished for the sake of effect, and far removed from life as I had experienced it, growing up in those very surroundings. The annoyance never abated until years later when I returned for a visit and was completely overcome by my own reactions to all that I saw and felt. I did not recall being overwhelmed by these same conditions when I had lived there. But now my responses seemed to echo in self-indicting fashion those I had heard described by eyes to whom it was foreign.

The same holds true for a westerner who has lived in the East and returns to the West years later. All of a sudden, definitions of wants and needs take on new points of reference. Priorities all become rearranged. Sometimes there is more justification in the surprise reaction of unfamiliarity than there is in the desensitization that comes from immersion. We all remember the old story of the frog that is gradually boiled to death. When placed in a cauldron of cold water that is gradually heated to boiling, the frog continues to swim in comfort, oblivious to what is happening. If, on the other hand, the same frog is dropped into boiling water, it immediately leaps out for its safety. The gradual change went unnoticed, accommodated beyond reason, while the drastic change met with self-preserving common sense.

Undeniably, being part of a culture brings about a level of comfort with the ways and means by which people live. But that familiarity does not guarantee sensitivity or objectivity. Proximity is not synonymous with understanding. Indeed, the very nearness we experience through modern technology may make us *more* vulnerable to distortion and victimization. The ideas and personalities the media thrust upon our imaginations subtly condition our consciousness in ways that even political totalitarianism cannot accomplish. We are unavoidably beguiled, in this so-called postmodern world, to an unprecedented degree. The constant bombardment of images shapes the perceptions of a whole generation and results in altered beliefs and lifestyles that make even the aberrant seem normal. The double-edged tragedy is not only that we are *in* such an environment but any warning that we are being molded possibly for the worse is contemptuously mocked as insane.

INFORMED BY UNDERSTANDING

Since every person is in the grasp of this cultural thrust, understanding what is happening to us as a civilization becomes critical or we risk a destiny of alarming possibilities. At any given time, minds are almost certainly at work at a feverish pace—penning modern-day versions of *Mein Kampf* or *Das Kapital*, plotting new worlds to conquer or old hates to avenge, conjuring new technologies to make our present attainments dissatisfying and obsolete. Some movie mogul somewhere is probably discussing a script that will tear away at any last vestige of reverence still residing in the human heart. Some new weapon may be in the works that could bring the world to its knees, at the mercy of a despot. And while all these possibilities loom, none of us knows what new diseases, atrocities, or tragedies await us at the turn of the next century.

Immersed in this mix of change and decay, can we at least understand the scope of the conflict? Can we appeal to our collective conscience while a few still remain who realize that there must be fences in life, else predators, with unrestrained and insatiable passions, will break down every wall of protection and relentlessly plunder everything we treasure?

Bearing in mind that we are not only *near* to this cultural explosion but are also, in fact, *in* it, the first step is that of diagnosis. What is it we are supposed to be near to and immersed in? The answer may at first seem to be protracted, but a simplistic approach for the sake of brevity only adds to the shallowness that is symptomatic of our crisis of thought. When a cultural mind-set has cut deeply into one's life, the correctives must also be deep.

After this step is completed we will not only understand the mystery of wickedness but we might well be jolted by the reality of the molding and manipulative power of culture over each of us. Only this depth of analysis will help us to understand why we make certain decisions or choose certain lifestyles. An awareness of the profound impact of culture can be a rude awakening but a necessary one. It not only reveals the rationality or irrationality of our reasons; it also exposes the inevitable consequences of the choices we make, consequences we might wish to escape but find to be unalterable.

EVICTING THE SACRED

One of the symptoms of modern and postmodern change is our large stock of new words, or certainly the new use of old words—terms such as *user-friendly, downsizing, multiculturalism, politically-correct, homophobic, postmodern, poststructuralism,* and *deconstruction.* If the cartographers of our time are working away furiously to draw up new maps as countries emerge and dissolve daily, our neologists (those who coin new words) are having a field day. One such word that we are all now accustomed to hearing repeatedly is *secular*, or *secularization*. Despite its familiarity, I suspect that many of us would find ourselves stumbling when asked to define what this word really means.

The word itself has a broad sweep and in differing contexts brings a different spin to the central idea. For our purposes we will concentrate on its social implications. Secularization is one of the most powerful conditioning influences in cultural formation today. Virtually every major decision that affects our mind-molding institutions—even in the highest offices of the land—is made on the basis of a secularized world-view. This factor, more than anything else, is the vantage point behind the emotionally charged debates that are at the forefront of Western life and, to varying degrees, of life in other parts of the world as well.

What does secularization really mean? With a touch of humor and an edge of sarcasm, the following lines summarize this new reigning world-view.

> First dentistry was painless.
> Then bicycles were chainless,
> Carriages were horseless,
> And many laws enforceless.
> Next cookery was fireless,
> Telegraphy was wireless,
> Cigars were nicotineless,
> And coffee caffeineless.
> Soon oranges were seedless,
> The putting green was weedless,
> The college boy was hatless,
> The proper diet fatless.
> New motor roads are dustless,
> The latest steel is rustless,
> Our tennis courts are sodless,
> Our new religion—godless.[1]

A secular world-view is admittedly and designedly the underlying impetus that presently propels Western culture. As the poem artfully reminds us, secularization assumes that this world—the material world—is all we have. To uncover and explain how this came about is a historian's challenge and a sociologist's occupation. The hard reality is that secularism is the philosophy of choice for American intellectual and political life. Any view that affirms the supernatural is, by definition, considered irrelevant or irrational. Secularism, or "saeculum," is implicitly "this worldly."

Peter Berger, the renowned sociologist and director of the Institute for the Study of Economic Culture at Boston University, defines secularization as "the process by which sectors of society and culture are removed from the domination of religious institutions and symbols." He expands on this in the following way:

> When we speak of society and institutions in modern western history, of course, secularization manifests itself in the evacuation by the Christian churches of areas previously under their control or influence as in the separation of Church and State . . . or in the emancipation of education from ecclesiastical authority. When we speak of culture and symbols, however, we imply that secularization is more than a social-structural process. It affects the totality of cultural life and of ideation, and may be observed in the decline of religious content in the arts, in philosophy, in literature and, most important of all, in the rise of science as an autonomous, thoroughly secular perspective on the world.[2]

Berger's choice of words is very interesting indeed, and the wide range that his lines encompass is of enormous importance. "The evacuation of the church" speaks of a fleeing body while "the emancipation of education" describes the liberation of the enshackled mind. All of the images stirred up are emotionally charged and are alluring as a study in themselves. Simply stated, secularism asserts that public life is to be conducted without reference to religion or to any notion of transcendence. This mood, as innocent and even as attractive as it seems in our modern day, has become the first step on the road to unmanageable evil. We will see that mood clearly as the idea is expounded. So let us get to the root of it, for here evil makes its entry through an innocent theory that moves so wrongheadedly.

GENTLE WORDS, HARSH REALITIES

Social analyst Os Guinness defines secularization as "the process by which religious ideas, institutions, and interpretations have lost their social significance." Herein lies both the heart and the will of the issue as crafted by the protagonists of secularism. Religious ideas have been knocked senseless in the social arena by the gladiators of the intellect. This is indeed stronger language than terms like *evacuation*. For some of the more aggressive secularists, the public humiliation and eradication of all religious belief would even be the goal. In the marketplace of ideas secularization claims to operate like free enterprise, with all points of view, even religious ones, vying equally for acceptance. In reality, however, religion has been systematically eliminated from public policy debates by an entrenched, highly secularized information elite.

The contention being made here—that this is not a mild-mannered drawing of the lines but, more accurately, a hostile takeover—is not even slightly overstated. Those who have carefully looked at our moral struggles universally acknowledge this philosophical attack upon the moorings of contemporary society. One has only to read the polemical overtones in the writings of Stephen J. Gould of Harvard, Richard Dawkins of Oxford, Carl Sagan of Cornell, and Eric T. Pengelley of the University of California at Davis to understand that the ridicule of a theistic framework is unblushingly overt. The success of secularization in keeping religious convictions out of the public arena is touted in vengeful terms. Science has vanquished theology. Reason has embarrassed faith.

As a test of this thesis, imagine with me the following scenario. A volatile moral issue that divides the nation is being discussed on prime-time television by a panel of experts. The panel is comprised of an educator, a philosopher, a civil libertarian, a politician, a lawyer, a journalist, and a minister. Who would be considered by the listening audience to be the most biased or "irrelevant" on the subject and therefore the least credible? Without a doubt, it would be the minister.

As much as one would seek to be conciliatory and work around this unfair bias, it is foolish to deny its existence. In academia, and even more so in the media, anyone in ministry today is more often than not ridiculed. To speak from a Christian perspective is frequently to become a target for abuse and hostility. The title "Reverend," especially if borne by a conservative, denotes anything but scholarship. Secularists, on the other hand, are assumed to be either well informed or transcendingly objective or both. They supposedly have no hidden agendas, no ulterior motive of making society conform to their repressive views. It is the religious who are bigoted and prejudiced and seek to crush the culture under their tyrannical heels.

When religious ideas are discussed, they are most often depicted as oppressive or antiquated. Seven decades after the Scopes trial, religionists who took part in that event are still the butt of the rationalists' ridicule. Those who believe in God as the author of the universe are dismissed as intellectual dinosaurs who have outlived their usefulness and ought graciously to cease to exist. They often find themselves the objects of witch hunts that seek to destroy belief in the sacred and portray religious belief as unwelcome and prejudicial. "Let us show God-talk for what it is," these militant secularists say, "full of ignorance and repression, signifying hate and intolerance." Not surprisingly, therefore, students entering college are very guarded about their religious beliefs for fear of being outcasts in the world of learning.

HOW DID WE GET HERE?

This is a radical inversion, is it not? Once it was the church that blazed new trails in education. Once the halls of learning were founded by religious leaders. Now, in a strange twist, secular powers charge that it is religious exploitation that has brought about our present situation; therefore it is payback time.

How this state of affairs came to be is important to understand. Let us look at it in two stages. We will first trace the evolution of secularism from being merely a voice among many vying for allegiance to becoming the reigning mind-set with the power to grant or ban the admissibility of all other views. In the second stage we will fully consider the ultimate destination of secularization in its logical outworking. The latter is felt by us in practical terms while the former—the analysis of the antecedents of the secularist mood—is unwittingly ignored as purely academic. To be fair and accurate, both aspects are important if one is to examine the subject and counter the situation with intelligence. The causes and results are with us today. To fully understand our situation and to appreciate the strengths and weaknesses of the secular perspective, we must examine both sides of the issue. Much may be learned from this social theory.

Our focus in this instance will be the secularization of America, because we see within this nation one of the high points of Western culture and the self-destructive downside that results if a secularized world-view becomes sovereign in matters of moral direction. We must come to grips with that ultimate end. It will not do to talk of evil as a result while ignoring its brain trust, the cause. Reality does not play mind games. What is more, if the mind is anesthetized in order to abort what comes to birth when wrong ideas are conceived in the womb of culture, the very life-giving force of the nation that nurtures that idea will die as well. When life is lost it does little good to cry out, "I think I've killed her!"

Three

The High Noon
of Promise

HOW DID the present American attitudes take form? Sociologists are careful to point out that the answer to that question will vary depending on one's philosophical starting point. If one thinks our contemporary cultural shift is all for the good, then the answer is arguably more pragmatic. If, on the other hand, the present is portrayed as all bad, then the answer is more philosophical. The truth is somewhere in the middle. For our purposes, therefore, we must approach this important subject of why we think the way we do on so many life-defining issues from at least three points of entry—the philosophical, the sociological, and most importantly, from the spiritual dimension. From these vantage points the pragmatic can be better understood.

Spanish scholar Julian Marias, who profoundly understood America even in its modern manifestations, once said:

> The United States is one of the great creations of history, like Rome or the Spanish Empire, realities which we enthusiastically study and understand today. . . . And the United States is being created before our very eyes, at an accelerated rate that allows us to observe it within our

lifetime, or even in less than a lifetime. . . . Is this not an intellectually exciting spectacle? Has there been a greater social and historical experiment available for man's contemplation in many centuries?[1]

He is right. How great and how exhilarating are the ideas embodied in this nation called the United States of America. Whatever else may be said of it, it is truly one of the most notable creations of history, born out of the amalgam of an enriching diversity. That is why millions come here to make it their home, aware, nonetheless, of its flaws and weaknesses. It is a dream in the eyes of the world's oppressed, and it was a dream in the making for its founding fathers. What, in the enfleshing of its vision, one may ask, was America "created" for? What provides this "intellectually exciting spectacle"?

The late Russell Kirk, the much-respected scholar, answered this question after years of research. As he brought his lengthy and well-argued case to an end in the closing pages of his book *The Roots of American Order*, he drew heavily from a lesser known American author, Orestes Brownson. (It should be added that Brownson's critically acclaimed book *The American Republic*, alongside his other writings, caused Lord Acton to remark that Brownson was probably the most penetrating American thinker of his day. That is a remarkable compliment, bearing in mind that he was a contemporary of writers like Melville, Emerson, and Hawthorne.) Blending his thoughts with those of Brownson, Kirk said:

> The United States was not brought into being to accomplish the work of socialism. For every living nation, Brownson wrote in *The American Republic*, "has an idea given it by providence to realize, and whose realization is its special work, mission, or destiny." The Jews were chosen to preserve traditions, and so that Messiah might arise; the Greeks were chosen for the realizing of art, science, and philosophy; the Romans were chosen for the developing of the state, law, and jurisprudence. And the Americans, too, have been appointed to a providential mission, continu-

amalgam - mixture, combination

ing the work of Greece and Rome, but accomplishing yet more. *The American Republic is to reconcile liberty with law.*[2]

Some will take issue with Kirk's invocation of a transcendent destiny assigned to America, implied by his words "appointed" and "chosen." However, the idea of a national "higher call" is not unique to the United States but has often been expressed by those from other nations. William Blake, for example, in his Romantic notions for England's destiny, said:

> And did those feet in ancient time
> Walk upon England's mountains green:
> And was the holy Lamb of God
> On England's pleasant pastures seen!
>
> I will not cease from Mental Flight,
> Nor shall my Sword sleep in my hand:
> Till we have built Jerusalem
> In England's green and pleasant Land.[3]

Mystics, or even visionaries, may be pardoned for invoking divine national purpose, because in a real sense nationhood needs its beacons and its paths to impart a sense of mission to its people. For America, in particular, her quest is poignantly defined in the noble but difficult pursuit of reconciling liberty with law. "Confirm thy soul with self-control, thy liberty with law" was not just poetic license. It was the vision. It was the dream. It was the central idea. It is not an accident of American history, therefore, that to this very day the nation is embroiled in debates over rights of privacy versus legislative authority. Morality, freedom, self-determination, happiness, sexuality, and security are all personal in their application. But nationally, they impinge upon the legislative role of government as it makes liberties possible for the protection of each and the benefit of all.

VISIONS OF POWER

The seemingly insurmountable struggle to reconcile liberty with law generated volumes of literature from eighteenth-century thinkers, whose writings provided the intellectual resource that positioned the individual as the peerless sovereign in the universal landscape. Their estimate of humanity's reasoning capacity formed the basis for their confident predictions of the future. But their hope that the light of reason could resolve every divisive issue was disappointed, for revolutions of a different nature were lurking in the shadows of the future for which reason alone would not be sufficient.

If the eighteenth century can be pictured as the intellectual looking in the mirror and becoming entranced by his or her own reflection like Narcissus of old, the nineteenth century by its end can be portrayed as one looking toward the horizon and being wooed by the mirage of the pragmatist. The encouraging smile of pragmatism—the philosophy of doing whatever works—beguiled many into opting for a world-view that in the long run simply doesn't work. The eighteenth century brought a confidence that exalted "rational man." The nineteenth century sounded the buzz and hum of machines that announced the arrival of "technical man." How could this combination of enlightened humanity and technical humanity have produced anything but the enfleshing of the age-old dream of utopia?

In retrospect, one would have thought that the bloodletting occasioned by the Indian mutiny in its revolt against the British (1857–1858), and India's attempt to shake off Western power, and the terrifying toll of the American Civil War (1861–1865), a raging conflict within a Western power, would have blunted the utopian hopes of the West. The reasonable response would have been to rethink humanity's self-confidence and narcissistic self-worship and to admit that the mind untamed by decency would imperil the process of law seeking to inform liberty. But the tug and attraction of the cerebral capacity with its inventive power overrode any philosophical caution that called for an examination of the person behind the machine. With blatant self-deception the assumption was made that mankind could be trusted with any instrument. Technological genius introduced an array of implements on civilization's field of dreams for the new games that would keep the imagination limitlessly entertained.

Undaunted, therefore, by the human toll in death and destruction that spelled caution, the Western dream was most dramatically expressed in the Great Exhibition of 1851. This exposition, for which the historic Crystal Palace was built in London, presaged the scientific triumphs that would define the march of the West into the future.

Hailing this occasion, the *Edinburgh Review* declared the accumulation of inventive genius under one roof as mankind's opportune moment: "to seize the living scroll of human progress, inscribed with every successive conquest of man's intellect." Historian John Warwick Montgomery insightfully draws attention to the most representative exhibit in the Crystal Palace, the model of a train that laid its own track. This curiosity symbolized the then existent mind-set, not just scientifically but philosophically, as mankind was on the move with built-in durability. In a very real sense a new road was being built to redefine the destination. This would be the classic "City of Man":

> The train that laid its own track can be regarded as the arch-symbol of the 19th century mind: the horizontal equivalent of pulling oneself to heaven by one's own bootstraps. For a train to have any advantage over an ordinary conveyance, its tracks must be so firmly anchored— independent of the train—that the train can build up great speed while safely relying on their stability. A train that lays its own track and takes it up again would have no superiority over a vehicle not running on tracks at all, for its tracks would be no more solidly anchored than the train itself. This was the 19th century: trying to lay its own tracks through technological inventiveness, achieving only pseudo-stability, and blind to the crash that will inevitably destroy all individual and societal engineers who refuse to let Christ provide a stable track for their lives.[4]

The self-contained train was the metaphor of self-sufficient man. The built-in capacity of power and provision, of overpowering and undergirding, was the envisioned reality ahead. From that day to this, pragmatism has been the handmaiden of secularized living: "We can do it."

IDEAS OF CHANGE

While technology was blazing the trail for humanity with tools for the future, Charles Darwin was unveiling humanity's primordial past. Science, in fact, was elbowing its way into becoming the sole interpreter of the past and the sufficient hope for the future. As confidence in humanity's creative capacity was increasing, confidence in God's creative power was diminishing. In keeping with the metaphysical mood, therefore, Marxism, avowedly atheistic and politically repressive, was spawned at this time, dehumanizing millions in its wake. Paradoxically, while espousing atheism, Karl Marx in small measure understood the human capacity for a destructive self-centeredness. He worked furiously, therefore, to ensure that the worker not be lost in the whirlwind of technological gains. His ideology called for the employer and the employee to march together to their classless society. How pathetic was his utopian zeal, for it instead provided the philosophical womb that birthed some of history's most dastardly crimes.

The change in the cultural landscape was patently clear. The human mind was becoming the factory of cultural retooling, gaining its impetus from scientific theory, which worked itself into political theory and finally into our value systems. It was only a matter of time before social engineers would demand a rebuilding of the philosophical framework underlying national morality. Amid the victorious cheers of the new horizons within humanity's reach, the voice of God and the way of Christ were summarily discarded. The bright lights on the outside ignored the disfigurement and indeed, the darkening within. The tracks of technology prepared the way for the engines of reason and the shunting of the spirit. Destined for the secular city, those along for the ride courted the intellect while ignoring the longings of the heart. That mistake is deadly: Any cultural imperative that obstinately refuses to understand the human heart lives with an irrationality that breeds the monstrosities we have witnessed in this century.

This "seizing the living scroll of human progress," as the *Edinburgh Review* described it, locked step with the conquering march of science and left its mark on the American mind. Secularism as a sociopolitical theory—this worldliness—was taking shape, born from the fusion of brain and machine with disregard for the soul.

But this, interestingly enough, is only the recent past. Technological capacity was not the sole progenitor of the American mind. One can readily understand how and why such enthusiasm could take hold of human imagination. Inventive and pragmatic genius are recent attainments and accomplishments that can induce a sense of creative self-sufficiency. But for the West there had been a more distant past that should have tempered that philosophical hope. There were traits in her character and knowledge that harked back to a people who also had envisioned a glorious future. An understanding of that imprint provides an even more fascinating tale and reveals the grandeur and vulnerability of human intellect in its progressivistic march.

CONCEPTS OF OLD

Even prior to the great scientific accomplishments that have led to the present, the philosophical ideas that made these creations possible had already been imparted into America's national character. This is of extraordinary importance to note, because the mind-set that existed in the formative years of this nation provided the soil to nurture the ideas that, in turn, made modern technology possible. But if the mind-set that led to our discoveries has since changed drastically, then those very advancements that now provide our strengths become liabilities and can destroy their "creators," becoming in their hands the deadliest instruments of evil. The *soil* of the Western mind into which the seeds of scientific gains were sown made what was previously only a possibility an actuality for this generation. But now, secularism dangerously flirts with contaminating the moral soil that had helped sprout her gains. It is pivotal, therefore, for those of us who are the inheritors of this new world to come to terms with the "ancestral" traits that fathered this nation and to examine the soil that nurtured those ideas.

Kirk brings a wealth of fascinating information to bear on this discussion, arguing that there are at least four cities, or cultures, that have left their indelible marks upon the Western world in general and upon America in particular. The American mind, he rightly says, has resulted from the confluence of Athens, Rome, Jerusalem, and London.

The Greeks have given to us our philosophical categories; the Romans have given to us much in our legal categories; the Hebrews have provided a base for our moral categories; and the English have given us our very language and the principles of representative government. (One may add to England's bequest architecture, institutes of learning, and a wealth of other strengths.) Many who ignore this heritage do so, not so much out of willfulness, as from a chronic disinterest in history. A knowledge and appreciation of history is difficult for a culture so enthralled by the moment, a culture that shuns the discipline of a larger context in any study. Unfortunately this loss of historical interest has made the present difficult to address because the context of the past is imperative if we are to salvage the future.

I remember sitting next to a young man at the fiftieth anniversary celebration of a church. After enduring about fifteen minutes of "I remember when" speeches, he turned to me and muttered, "I hate all this nostalgia stuff." I paused and then whispered, "The only thing worse than nostalgia is amnesia."

The story is told of a Western diplomat a few years ago who found himself seated next to Chinese premier Chou Enlai. Unable to make much conversation with this disconcertingly quiet state leader, he finally said to Premier Chou, "What do you think of the French Revolution?" Chou paused for what seemed an interminable silence and then said, "It's too soon to tell." Such, I fear, is the diametric difference in perspective; the East finds a two-hundred-year span too short while the West finds fifty years too distant. How easy is it, then, for the modern reader to care for cultures of two millennia ago and recognize how definitive such a study can be for us? But the information gleaned can actually be stirring to the soul if it is studied well.

For the sake of a little self-knowledge, which is indispensable, let us take a cursory look at just one of the cultures that molded our early soul. Even a brief glance yields a challenging lesson. In Greece we may well see our own reflection. But while recognizing the classic grandeur of its legitimate glory, we must resist the temptation to be enamored too long by the image. For it was a glory that was ultimately dissipated by a colossal spiritual blind spot.

INFLUENCES THAT SHAPED US

"It's all Greek to me" is our common way of saying something is incomprehensible. Yet, if we look carefully at the roots of common English words, we will see how much we have gained from the Greeks, even in our conceptual framework. We speak of an elaborate argument, rich in words but impoverished in ideas, as mere *sophistry*—an ostentatious verbal display intended to impress and deceive. This comes from the Greek philosophers, the Sophists, who were known for their skill in argumentation that employed a fallacious use of logic.

Or, we speak today of *agoraphobia*, a fear of open spaces, which originates in a reference to the Greek open-air markets, called the Agora. We might talk of being *stoical* in the face of tragedy, meaning a grim endurance without emotional display. The Stoic philosophers held that wisdom lay in rising above passion and in unperturbed submission to the divine will.

Much has been written on the legendary splendor of Greece, and indeed the West owes an unpayable debt to this great civilization and culture that in its halcyon days knew tremendous glory, a glory that continues to inspire even through its ruins. Lord Byron eulogized her, "Fair Greece! Sad relic of departed worth! Immortal, though no more; though fallen, great!" Milton acclaimed Athens "the eye of Greece, mother of arts and eloquence." Johann Goethe extolled, "Of all the peoples the Greeks have dreamt the dreams of life best." Percy Bysshe Shelley lyricized, "'Let there be light!' said Liberty, and like the sunrise from the sea, Athens arose!" Dionysius Solomos, the nineteenth-century thinker, intoned, "Enclose in your soul Greece . . . and you shall feel every kind of grandeur." Modern historian Edith Hamilton surmised, "They [the Greeks] were the first westerners; the Spirit of the West, the modern spirit, is a Greek discovery, and the place of the Greeks is in the modern world." And Sir Henry Maine wrote in 1876, "Except the blind forces of nature, nothing moves in this world which is not Greek in its origin."

The Greeks came very close to conquering the whole world. But if their own writers of antiquity had penned the story of Greece, they might well have portrayed her glory and demise in microcosm through the person of Alexander the Great. It was said that even if he had conquered the world he would still not have attained contentment, for he was his own worst rival. A daring general in military warfare and a student of Aristotle, he made great gains in his attempt to unify the world under Greek thought, though he was not able to find unity in his own life.

And that represents the ultimate Greek tragedy. Today the fallen stones of its once legendary cities tell the tale of a former splendor; in reality the "great age" of Athens lasted less than fifty years.

While the Greek experience in politics and government was known and studied by many of America's founding fathers, it was more in the arts and philosophy that Greece was to leave its mark on America. The names of Socrates, Plato, and Aristotle are familiar to modern university students. Their concepts of virtue, Plato's *Republic*, Aristotle's *Ethics*, and Socratic maxims are woven into an understanding of Western philosophy.

But it is here that our attention ought to be really piqued, because in the American experience there was both a borrowing and a refusing of Greek culture. For example, the Greek concept of the Academy and her systematization of knowledge has helped to shape the study of the major disciplines in America. Ideas that originated in Greece were sifted via Rome through European medieval culture and carried from there into America. In fact, even predating that, so much of Hellenic thought had entered the world of New Testament times that the apostle Paul singularly addressed those issues in the Scriptures. Paul's teaching on the soul, on sin, and on the afterlife was done in such terminology that the Greeks would be hard-pressed to miss both the relevance of the Christian message to Greek thought as well as its contradistinction. Augustine's *The City of God* can never be fully appreciated without an understanding of Platonic teaching. The medieval church was heavily instructed in the works of Aristotle.

THE RELATIVISM THAT KILLED

But it is here that we must pause and ask why this glory was so short-lived. What brought about the ultimate ruin of this, the mother of the arts and invention? These questions have much to say to America in her struggle with wickedness today.

It was the Sophists who popularized Protagoras's phrase "Man is

the measure of all things" and translated it to mean that individuals
are not responsible to any transcendent moral authority for their actions. Aristotle had taught that the three principal reasons for knowledge were Truth, Morality, and Technique (technology), in that
order—what is true, how to live, and the instrumental use that this
knowledge could serve. The warning from philosophy is powerful.
Kirk forthrightly describes the death knell that sounded the demise
of this great nation.

> It was the clear relativism of the Sophists, not the mystical insights of
> Plato, nor Aristotle's aspiration after the Supreme Good, which domi-
> nated the thinking of the classical Greeks in their decadence. The failure
> of the Greeks to find an enduring popular religious sanction for the or-
> der of civilization had been a main cause of the collapse of the world of
> the polis.[5]

This may be the most important sociophilosophic pronouncement
for America to learn. Even though scholars tire of hearing it, the
truth of Alexis de Tocqueville's statement is hard to ignore. The
famed French thinker repeatedly said it was America's religious bond,
which was stronger than that of either Rome or Greece, that held her
together.

Perhaps a very simple but poignant legend told of Alexander the
Great illustrates the point. It is said that when he was dying at
Babylon, Alexander crawled out of his tent on all fours at midnight,
intending to drown himself in the Euphrates River. He hoped his
body would be lost and that men would then believe that he was, in
truth, immortal. But his attempt failed. His wife brought him back to
die in his bed, and posterity would laugh at that attempt by one who
conquered the world but lived under such a self-deluding and farcical notion.

Alexander could not accept his human limitations, and as he toyed
with playing god he was dragged back to his chambers to die as a
man, out of control. The Greeks had long believed that the very con-

cept of human excellence could be pursued only if man's purpose was first known. Purpose and performance had to be tied together. But purpose had been lost, and technique and pleasure had replaced truth and morality. The pragmatic plague of "how to build" became more important than "how to be." Under the debris of the pillars and the stones is not just the story of a civilization destroyed by internecine wars but of a people who would not acknowledge the wretchedness and evil pent up within the human heart and the absolute necessity that man find a measure outside of himself. It was not long before preoccupation with a perfect body overtook the warning cry of an imperfect heart and soul.

America's scientists and artists need only to look back at Greece to realize what happens when technological genius and unbridled imagination become ends in themselves. Artistic liberty multiplied by technological capacity produces a modern-day Greece fashioned with American ingenuity. The old America had the mind to sift through these strengths and harness them. The new America finds itself without a point of reference. An extremely vocal and domineering influence in our culture, the arts are now energized with distributive power for global impact. On the part of some, art itself has become just a euphemism for deviance and discord, creating alternate realities in its path and perverting the popular imagination as it runs roughshod over every virtue. Purpose and performance have been severed, and performance is now judged in the free-fall zone of artistic vacuum, totally unsecured by the safety net of human essence. The cultural train that is laying its own tracks is derailing an entire nation, and the screams of the victims of the resulting evil call out for help.

THE DEFINITIVE DIFFERENCE

In its early days, though philosophically indebted to Greece, America also had a fundamental ideational difference. Greece's noblest phi-

losophers merely nudged us in the direction of an ultimate mind to
which we must look. But America did not stop there, for she knew
what the autonomous heart could engender and what it needed from
God Himself. The first line ever printed in North America was in the
New England Primer, and it read, "In Adam's fall we sinned all." That
man had fallen was at least given popular consent, some credence.
The human heart was deemed to be in need of instruction in moral
uprightness. There needed to be a renewing of the mind.

Today, however, such sentiment has been angrily and mockingly
denounced in academia; laden down by our technology, we crawl to
our halls of fame like Alexander, desperately wanting the world to
believe that we, too, are immortal. How revealing it is that in the
bloodiest century of history we deny human depravity. The relativism
of ancient Greece has worked its way into modern America, though
the Greek philosophers themselves, even in their day, warned that
relativism would be suicidal. To her credit, early America knew that
this was not merely a philosophical problem, as real as that was. This
was a problem of the soul, and the heart of humanity was in need of
redemption.

Today we have gone backward. We deny both the spiritual and the
philosophical. And our end result will be the same as ancient Greece.
The imprint of Greece is upon us and upon the new soil of American secularism. It is said of Greece that it is not that the people were
abandoned by their gods because they had become so wicked but that
they abandoned their gods because their gods had become too
wicked. In our time, the gods of relativism who shape our ideas may
well be in the same mold and worthy of abandonment if we are to
avert the debacle that overtook the Greek soul.

A brief look at the philosophical influence of Greece clearly reveals
at least one component of American culture. But even here, early
America knew both her legitimate heritage and what she would not
borrow. Centuries have passed, and as America has grown and waxed
strong, the belief that was once rejected—that man is the measure of

all things—is now espoused. The conviction that was once held—the
fallen nature of men—is now rejected. And in every sense of the term,
a major conflict for cultural control has begun to emerge. On the one
hand there is the cry for liberty from the superintendency of law over
private practice. On the other hand the same voices call upon the law
to ban the assumptions of the Christian truths of the fall of man and
of mankind's redemption. And the Christian, bewildered by this dramatic turn, sees the darkening horizon because of the encroaching
deformity within the cultural soul. The call of the Supreme Artist,
who created all things beautiful, is being mocked. Secularism has
grabbed its philosophical knife to silence the Artist in the public
square. But the memory of where the nation first began still haunts,
and the evil being evidenced is painful. The heart and mind cry out
in prayer.

> O God of earth and altar, bow down and hear our cry,
> Our earthly rulers falter, our people drift and die;
> The walls of gold entomb us, the swords of scorn divide,
> Take not thy thunder from us, but take away our pride.
> From all that terror teaches, from lies of tongue and pen,
> From all the easy speeches that comfort cruel men,
> From sale and profanation of honor and the sword,
> From sleep and from damnation, deliver us, good Lord.
> Tie in a living tether the prince and priest and thrall,
> Bind all our lives together, smite us and save us all;
> In ire and exultation, aflame with faith and free,
> Lift up a living nation, a single sword to thee.[6]

THE VISION IMPERILED

The despairing words of the poet Wordsworth as he saw England on
the same slippery slope will translate well onto the American scene:

Milton! Thou shouldest be living at this hour.
England hath need of thee: She is a fen
Of stagnant waters: Altar, sword and pen,
Fireside, the heroic wealth of hall and bower
Have forfeited their ancient English dower
Of inward happiness. We are selfish men;
Oh! raise up. Return to us again;
And give us manners, virtue, freedom, power.[7]

As stated earlier, it has been common in history for nations to see themselves as a context in which the cities of men do battle with the City of God. And in that sense the conflict between *soulcraft* and *statecraft*[8] is not new. Keats has said the world is a "vale of soul-making." But in America it has reached unprecedented proportions because the whole drift into secularization has, by virtue of modern capacity, touched every area of life, from womb to tomb.

There are no signs of letup, and the philosophy now undergirding the interpretation of law implicitly denies the soul. The destiny-defining consequences have moved from a philosophical theory to a social reality from which we seek deliverance. It is that sociological understanding of the road to the present that next occupies our attention.

Four

The Storms of Conflict

STORIES HAVE a way of making the rounds, especially if they have a good punch line. One such story told and retold in India describes a rich man who sought to buy up an entire village. The man walked from house to house, offering a disproportionately large sum of money to each householder in exchange for his property. Delighted at the prospect of such a large profit, all readily entered into the sale except for one determined old man who owned a small shack right in the center of the village. No sum of money would change his mind, and he responded to each increment offered with the calm rejoinder, "I'm not interested in selling."

Frustrated, the rich man finally had to be content to buy the whole village except for this tiny piece of real estate in the middle. The old man relished his symbolic victory. Every time the rich man had a visitor in the village, the old man stepped out of his little hut and, wagging his bony finger, tauntingly declared, "If he tells you he owns this whole village, don't believe him; this part right here in the middle still belongs to me."

There is a sad, yet striking similarity in this story to the church and her solace when conceding the cultural dominance of secularism over what was once religious terrain. The analogy is even heightened, for the transference of dominion has not been just of land but also of ideas. Retreating from the world, many Christians seek cover inside their church buildings, wagging their fingers at the "secular owner-ship" of the social landscape and receiving petty satisfaction in saying, "This little part still belongs to us." This is the way the dust has settled after the storms of conflict and the winds of change have raged over which central ideas should govern our culture.

BETRAYING A TRUST

Certain differences surface from a study of the changing moods to-ward the Christian faith in Western countries where there has always been freedom to proclaim the gospel. But there are also some strik-ing similarities. The directional shift away from Christianity was set in motion in the eighteenth and nineteenth centuries as the process of secularization was unmistakably under way. The storms of moral and cultural controversy that have raged in the twentieth century, tearing away at the core of Western culture, find their progenitors in these earlier eras.

There is no dearth of analysis in the scholarly world to attempt an explanation of the whys and hows of these social changes. Any debate that arises lies in the allocation and degree of responsibility attributed to the various carriers of such changes. The world was changing not just in capacity but in speed, and shifts were under way in every arena.

Canadian historian David Marshall lists the conditions that gradu-ally made the social climate in Canada inhospitable to the Christian message. These conditioning influences are not restricted to Canada alone. They are true for much of the West. The increase in scientific knowledge and the philosophy that was smuggled in with it, the shifting focus of intellectual life in its "this worldly" expertise, the rise of a consumer culture, the emergence of an urban industrial society, and the struggle of the church to cope with a rapidly changing world—all of these factors energized a world moving at high speed.

With such multidimensional agents of change it would be presumptuous to single out one exclusive cause that altered the mind of a whole society. But Marshall does take a bold step to point the finger. His conclusion may come as a surprise to the Christian who has left this subject unstudied. A vision of the prophet Nathan standing before King David and saying, "You are the man!" certainly comes to mind when we encounter Marshall's daring charge. Alarmingly, it may also be justifiable.

Marshall lays a major portion of the blame for the slide into secularism at the door of the Christian clergy. It was from their ranks, he says, that the defection began. From their ranks came the call to congregations to abandon the notion of an authoritative Scripture and surrender the biblical perspective on life's deepest questions. This was the explosive force that would demolish any claim to Christian uniqueness.

The point that Marshall makes is too vital to hastily bypass. It is of paramount importance to note that intellectuals across history have played key roles in the uprooting of one idea and the planting of another. The establishment of new orthodoxies by the intellectual elite and the dismantling of others is not as formidable a task when the desired change propelled by scholars appeals to the common person's autonomy while enthroning the elite at the same time.

The perilous blunder that society so often makes when it surrenders such an empowerment to the few is to assume that intellectuals always arrive at cultural deductions by virtue of open minds and scholarly objectivity. Surprisingly, and often, these groups bring an agenda all their own, and their motivation is anything but pristine. Was it not Aldous Huxley who admitted that he wanted this world to not have meaning so that he was freed to pursue his own erotic and political pursuits? One of the great temptations to intellectuals is to assume that in grabbing the finger of their own discipline they have grabbed the fist of reality. Specializing in one field, some are able to exploit that knowledge to interpret every other discipline as well. Their motives are not value-free. We must beware of the vulnerability of the many to be shaped in their thinking by the few whose narrow expertise becomes life-defining to the mainstream.

Here, then, is the terrible disappointment to Christians. Betrayal came from their own educated ranks as some in leadership succumbed to and even joined forces with skeptics, giving strength to the tentacles of secularism to gradually choke out religious life. Secularizing voices among the clergy berated the conservative authorities in institutions for not giving free vent to those of a liberal stripe. Once that openness was granted and liberals had gained power, those same voices countered with greater bigotry to block out any conservative view. Since then, there has been made, at best, a patronizing provision for the conservative as a marginalized viewpoint.

Marshall's thesis, singling out the clergy, is disheartening and incomprehensible to those who cherish their sacred call to ministry as stewards of the Word of God. But those from within the church who called for a watered-down scriptural authority hailed the capitulation of the Christian message to contrary philosophies as the triumph of reality over religion. Conservative scholars for whom the Scriptures were absolute were left with the staggering task of their defense—a monumental responsibility with limited access.

FORSAKING A CALL

With a sharper thrust but from a different angle, Peter Berger moves beyond the role of the clergy in the secularization of the world to the role of Protestantism as a whole. He concludes that in their preoccupation with "other worldliness" and in their emphasis on redemption as "personal and individual," Protestants unwittingly abandoned the arena of *this world* itself, leaving it a vacated venue. The "New Jerusalem" became the place of focus for them, and *this* world was relinquished to secular causes and activity. In effect, with "angels" no longer in this world, the astronomer and, indeed, the astronaut could now interpret space and time.

Does Berger single out Protestantism for that unique and dubious role in distinction to the rest of Christendom? Yes, he does. In contrast to Catholics, who still retained the mystery, the magic, and the miracle woven into the fabric of the world order, Berger says Protestants stripped the material world to bare matter and separated it totally from the world to come. The winds of irreligion gained momentum, unencumbered by a spiritual presence. The keys of the kingdom had been handed over.

As fascinating and true as these factors may be, there is very little doubt that one major idea or theory was ultimately to become the hatpin in the heart of Christian thought—a hatpin stuck in the heart of Christendom and buttressed by the rear guard of other advancing secular ideas. By the middle of the nineteenth century, what became known as "higher," or "historical criticism"—with roots in Germany—began to gain wider acceptance and do severe damage to scriptural authority. Though acceptable as a discipline, negative higher criticism prejudicially reduced the Bible to mere literature and created doubts about the authorship and authenticity of certain books of the Bible, especially the Gospels. This theory, clearly tendentious by its users, swept through Europe and Great Britain and stormed the institutes of higher learning in North America with equal devastation. Ultimately, it drew the life blood from the church.

The church was already caught in the context of economic, social, and academic change. Now, into that frame of reference the text of Scripture was brought under judgment. Suspect, and positioned as a piece of literature to be dissected and dismembered at the hands of scholars with unhidden pretexts, the Scriptures were well on their way to being dismissed as nothing more than ethnic utopianism punctuated with altruistic pronouncements. By stripping the Bible of divine authorship, liberal scholarship made it just another piece of literature, open to attack and critique. Its definitive roles for faith and conduct were debunked, and its injunctions were de-legitimized. Many who were determined to pursue this agenda dared to remain in the ministry and function within the church, all the while reducing its reason for existence to myth. This was a Copernican revolution within the church, and the signature of God upon the Scriptures was deemed a forgery. It was no longer a God-authored book, but a man-concocted collection.

This was no longer theology—from God to us—but anthropology—about us and our thoughts toward God. In short, the author of the Scriptures was renamed. If Marshall and Berger are even close to being right in their deductions, it is truly lamentable that secularism may have entered into such dominance with the help of the church.

One cannot overstate how important a social factor this was in secularizing Western consciousness. Had there been only the advancement of scientific theorizing and the socioeconomic changes, skeptics would still not have been able to mount a sufficient attack upon so many treasured beliefs. It took this extra step, this dizzying punch delivered from within the church itself, this attack upon the very mind and heart of the Christian message, the Bible, to make possible secularism's total victory.

Accompanying this devastating attack upon the Scriptures came a scramble for power. Inaugural addresses at seminaries and universities became predictable—the conservatives protesting that the Scriptures were being plundered, and the liberals hailing the victory of learning over superstition. Not accidentally, therefore, as the decade of the sixties dawned and the culture began to convulse against authority, *Christian Century* published a poem by Thomas C. Arthur entitled, "Death of Another Salesman."

Sooner or later the preacher
Wakes up to the fact
That he can't save *everybody*.

He may even think
That after all,
There is such a division
As the Elect.

If he goes on thinking
He may come to realize
That the "Elect" are inclined
To agree with him.

If by some chance
He contemplates still further,
He may find
That *some* of the damned
Have a *point*.

Then he may wonder
If *anyone at all* can be saved!
He might even count himself
Among the great mass
of the Lost.

He will then flounder about,
Snatching at slivers of truth.
He may even discover
That he can't swim.[1]

At first blush one may not realize how pitiful such a plunder of the message of Christ is when accomplished at the hands of those to whom it was entrusted. Somehow, a slow bleed and loss of philosophical strength does not seem as real to people as a sudden amputation. One of Christendom's most revered buildings serves as a very painful illustration of how tragic such self-mutilation can be to the

cause of Christ when the carriers of such division are within it. I refer to the Church of The Holy Sepulcher as it functions today in the
city of Jerusalem. Let me quote the words of the English writer
Arthur Leonard Griffith.

> At the center of the old city [Jerusalem] stands the Church of The Holy
> Sepulcher, reputedly on the sight of the original Calvary and the origi-
> nal Garden of The Resurrection. It stands, but only because ugly steel
> scaffolding permanently supports the walls inside and out. This church
> is one of the dirtiest, most depressing buildings in all Christendom. It
> should be torn down and rebuilt. This is not possible, however, because
> the Church of The Holy Sepulcher belongs jointly to the Abyssinians,
> Armenians, Copts, Greeks, Syrians and Roman Catholics, and their
> priests will hardly speak to one another, let alone cooperate in a joint
> enterprise of rebuilding. Each communion preserves its own separate
> chapel, and conducts its own ceremonies; and to make the situation lu-
> dicrous, the keys of the church have been entrusted to a family of Mus-
> lims who in order to answer the call of Allah five times daily, have turned
> the entrance into a Muslim Mosque. Nowhere in all the world can you
> find a more tragic symbol of the mutilation of Christ's body than the
> Church of The Holy Sepulcher in Jerusalem.[2]

The only difference between the Church of The Holy Sepulcher
and the self-defacing influence of those who attacked scriptural authority in Western Christendom is that the keys of the kingdom were
handed over to secular powers as the voice of God in the Scriptures
was silenced by those to whom it was entrusted.

REDEFINING REALITY

Common to the voices of both the liberal clergy and those hostile to
Christianity was their view of the supernatural. The shift from the sacred to the secular was undergirded by one fundamental idea that was
foisted upon Western culture: The implicit denial of the miraculous or
the supernatural to explain human essence or existence. It was clearly
acknowledged by all its detractors that the Christian message incorpo-

rated many great ideas. But intrinsic to all Christian orthodoxy is the belief that the world did not come about because of natural causes or means. Both in its creation and in its sustenance a supernatural entity is recognized. The entire existence of Israel as a nation, says the Old Testament, is by virtue of God's intervening hand: "I carried you on eagles' wings and brought you to myself. . . . I am the LORD your God, who brought you out of Egypt" (Exod. 19:4; 20:1).

The whole prophetic message pointed to the coming of One who would bring personal and cosmic redemption. In the New Testament, Jesus, who was born of a virgin (a truth believed even by Muslims), punctuated His life and message with the dramatic and instructive use of the miraculous. From the restoration of sight to the blind to the regeneration of the human heart—all was the work of God. Jesus' death on the cross and His resurrection from the dead attested to the authority and purpose for which He had come. The church was instituted as the "bride of Christ" to reflect His splendor and await His return, in the meantime, "occupying" until He came. The Bible is God-breathed, and as such it is the revelation to man of the mind of God and of His absolute standard for our lives.

All of this belief was leveled by the new winds blowing, winds that made "Thus says the Lord" an impossibility. The Bible itself was in question, and the world was reconstituted as a "brand-new creation" assembled by the minds of men riding upon the engines of change, marketed by the genius of consumer demand and licensed by the institutions of the state. As a result, it is no longer only land that is secularized but life itself. Matter is under the spotlight; the soul is systematically disfigured in the attic of existence.

MOCKING THE SACRED

The sequence that followed became predictable. The open mocking of the sacred by the modern critic culminated a long process of desacralizing life itself. First the world was denuded of transcendence, then the Scriptures were rendered irrelevant, and finally humankind was made nothing more than matter. In the name of progress and of supposed sensitivity to other systems of thought, much has been done to bully the Christian believer. The ravages of a diminished view of Scripture have gained even greater momentum, to the point of complete absurdity.

Few instances better illustrate this than one of the recent translations of the Bible. Referring to the Oxford University Press's release of a "culturally sensitive" version of the Bible, the religious editor of *Newsweek* recently quipped that the King James Bible "never looked so good before." These are his poignant comments:

> Readers who find the Bible sexist, racist, elitist and insensitive to the physically challenged, take heart. Oxford University Press's new "inclusive language version" of the New Testament and Psalms has cleaned up God's act. In this version, God is no longer "Father" and Jesus is no longer "Son." The hierarchical title of "Lord" is excised as an archaic way to address God. Nor does God (male pronouns for the deity have been abolished) rule a "kingdom"; as the editors explain, the word has a "blatantly androcentric and patriarchal character." . . . Even God's metaphorical "right hand" has been amputated out of deference to the left-handed. Some examples:
>
> - In the majestic opening of John's Gospel, "the glory he has from the Father as the only Son of the Father" becomes "the glory as of a parent's only child." (John 1:14)
>
> - The Lord's prayer now begins like this: "Father-Mother, hallowed be your name. May your dominion come." (Luke 11:2)
>
> - Jesus's own self-understanding as God's only son is generalized to: "No one knows the Child except the Father-Mother; and no one knows the Father-Mother except the Child . . ." (Matthew 11:27)
>
> - Avoiding another traditional phrase, "Son of Man," the Oxford text reads: "Then they will see 'the Human One' coming in clouds with great power and glory." (Mark 13:26)

The editors do not claim that Jesus spoke in gender-neutral language. But they obviously think he should have. The changes they have made are not merely cosmetic. They represent a fundamental reinterpretation of what the New Testament says—and how it says it. The King James Bible never looked so good.[3]

Truly noteworthy about such blatant ridicule is that it seems reserved only for the Christian. One is tempted to ask whether Oxford University Press would have dared to tamper with or so implicitly demean the Koran in this way. This single-minded attack on Christianity in the name of relevance underscores secularism's primary target. This translation has been done supposedly to achieve relevance—in principle, such an effort shows no more respect for the relevance of the Scriptures than it does for the claims of the Scriptures. No, such relentless attack upon anything that has to do with the supernatural is the imprint of secularist dogmatism.[4] To the secularist, the Bible cannot be the Word of God, for to grant even that theoretical possibility would be an admission of the supernatural. That concession by the postmodern person sold out to a naturalistic view of reality would be tantamount to the surrender of his or her world-view of a voiceless universe.

If this were all that secularism demonstrated we could accept it as a process that began two centuries ago and has now led to our social theory. But if the goal at the inception of America was to reconcile liberty with law, then we have reached a devastating contradiction. For law cannot merely serve as a random set of rules without any objective point of reference. And for law to be effective it is equally necessary that a reaction to its violation must go beyond an objective framework to a felt subjective response within the individual to whom the law is making its appeal. In other words, it is not sufficient just to have a law "out there" for people to obey. There must be an inner urge, or hunger, to keep and honor that law because it is good. Secularism cannot accomplish this in the hearts and minds of people, because the mind it has created is a pragmatic one, and pragmatism will always find ways to circumvent and misuse the law rather than to revere it.

Secularism criminally fails to measure up even theoretically to the purpose for which the nation was founded. It has done away with a moral law and destroyed the sensitivity of an individual toward honoring that law. The evil we now witness is from the ash heap of destroyed sensitivities. How that desensitization was accomplished we will further uncover. But this we know: Law and liberty can never be reconciled when external and internal constraints are arbitrary. How drastic that failure is, for it leads to the incredible eradication of one of society's greatest needs, which we will now address. This is a failure no nation can afford.

Five

The Twilight of Decency

A VILLAGE MAN was making his first visit to a big city. As he came closer to the teeming metropolis he was quite overwhelmed by the cars he saw moving past him at high speeds. Never having seen a car before, he scratched his head in puzzlement, wondering what made them run and wishing he had one of his own. How much better life would be if one could move at such speed, he thought.

Just at that moment, he noticed a car sputtering and fuming and jerking as it came to a stop. He observed the driver walk away and come back several moments later with a can in his hand. His curiosity piqued, he watched intently as the driver poured something from the can into the opening on the side of the car. Promptly thereafter, the car started again and sped on its way.

As the car disappeared he suddenly spied the tin can the driver had used, lying on the side of the road. With sheer delight he picked it up and let out a triumphant shout, "Now all I need is the thing that moves."

If the poor man wagging his finger at the rich landowner and saying, "This part still belongs to me," represents the beleaguered Christian in a secularized culture, the villager holding the empty gasoline can in the belief that all he needs now is the car represents the half-baked theory of secularism. It just does not work.

Secularism is a social theory holding the tin can of technology. The engine of civility is still eluding it. The question clearly has to be raised: If the supernatural is irrational, what will the secularist use as a point of reference for rationality? Who does one call upon for guidance in life's choices? Whose voice shall we hear on these issues, or is each one to depend on his or her own inner voice?

THE STRIPTEASE OF SECULARISM

After the wind and after the earthquake there came to the prophet Elijah living in the ninth century before the birth of Christ the comfort and direction of the still, small voice. In our current storm of controversy the silence is terrifying. There is no longer any voice, no more revelation "from above." Not only has secularization brought us a silent universe with no voice from without, it has also brought us a silence from within as it has redefined the whole role of conscience. It has removed any possibility of an objective supernatural revelation and supplanted it with the so-called inner voice of reason. It was only a matter of time before there would be no way to differentiate between the inner voice of reason and the inner promptings of unreason. Let me sustain this argument, because now we will see not merely the theoretical incoherence of secularism and its primary carriers; we will see that it leads to a pragmatism that is unworkable and an evil that is devastating.

As I have previously stated, implicit to the secularized world-view is not just the marginalization of any religious idea but its complete eviction from public credence in informing social policy. If an idea or a belief is "religiously based," be it in a matter of sexuality or marriage or education or whatever, then by that very virtue it is deemed unsuitable for public usage.

A definitive example of this public expulsion of religious ideas can be seen from two historic incidents in the city of Toronto, Canada. In the 1880s the mayor of that city was William Howland. Howland's platform, as he campaigned for office, was one of concern for the city's moral degeneration. He pledged to work toward making it a decent city and ridding it of some of the public vices and trades that victimized its people. His bid was successful, and he left as his legacy the still-used qualifier to the city of Toronto, "Toronto the Good."

Ironically, nearly a century later a major moral issue again caused political debate between candidates running for the mayor's post in Toronto. The incumbent was inundated with pleas to reconsider his position on the issue. He staunchly resisted that pressure, stating that most of those who were troubled by his stand were religiously minded people who, he said, "were prejudiced on such matters," and therefore, he would disregard their counsel.

That sweeping generalization of a position on a soul-testing, divisive, moral issue, patently dismissed as wrong because it is held by people who are also religious, is the cold hand and despising stance of secular consciousness. It has a self-blinding glare as it censors the rationality of religion. And it is indicative of the blatancy of the secularist's prejudice.

In the 1970s a leading entrepreneur who peddled hard-core pornography was brought to trial in a southern city of the United States. Most intriguingly, in the process of jury selection one of the questions posed of potential jurors by the defense attorney was whether or not they were members of a church. An affirmative answer to that value-laden question generally disqualified any juror in the eyes of the defense because "religious people have a prejudice against pornography." One can imagine how long it took in the South to find a jury so "uninfected" by the church that it could be "objective" on the matter of hard-core pornography.

But this was not the lowest point of it all—and it is here that the brains behind secularization manipulate the mind in matters that threaten decency. During the process of the trial the defense attorney resorted to a clever, indeed, intimidating line of questioning that disoriented and confused any witnesses against his client. The strategy ran as follows.

"Have you ever been into an art gallery?"

"Yes," would come the answer.

"Have you ever paid to go into an art gallery?"

"Yes," the witness would say again.

"Have you ever paid to go into an art gallery where there were paintings by the great masters of art?"

"Yes," once more the witness would repeat.

"Have you ever paid to go into an art gallery where there were paintings of unclothed people by the great masters?"

"Yes, I have," would come the hesitant reply as the witness would suddenly recognize that the predator was ready for the kill and there was no place to flee.

"Could you tell this jury," the derisive voice would thunder forth, "why you call what you paid to go and see 'art,' yet what my client sells you brand 'pornography'?"

With wringing hands, a confused mind, and a stuttering voice some meager philosophical banter would ensue—but the trap had been sprung. One could be absolutely certain that the worst possible answer in that secular courtroom would have been for an aged woman with hat and gloves and a cross hanging from her neck to have said, "Well, the Bible says that the body is the temple of God. . . ." The defense attorney could have rested his case with no further comment.

How irrational. How repressive. How irrelevant to the secularized consciousness is the invocation of a religious belief when establishing social moral boundaries and imposing them upon the ever-shifting soil of "community standards." But we may well ask from which side the imposition and irrationality *really* comes.

THE INDIGNITY OF NATURALISM

As I pondered this approach and argumentation thrust upon witnesses, it was obvious to me that they had clearly been placed in an indefensible position, because one cannot defend the particulars of a moral choice without first defending the theory in general upon which that choice is made. Secularism, on the other hand, can defend any choice because it is never compelled to defend its first principles, which are basically reduced to an antireligious bias. But secularists do not take into account that on their own terms no position needs to be defended if a commitment to it is sufficient reason in itself. If it is believed that all moralizing is purely one's private view then ought not that view itself be kept private? The secularist never answers how he or she determines whether anything is wrong with anything except by sheer choice. Secular belief grants itself privileges that it does not equally distribute.

That prejudice notwithstanding, let us consider the ploy behind the questioning in that courtroom and the possibility of unbridled evil that is created by implication. Secular theory has its self-preserving bag of tricks. When debating on any moral issue, secular thinkers delight in introducing some aberrant situation for which only two evil options are possible and forcing the absolutist to choose between them. By forcing those extreme solutions, they extrapolate the false deduction that there must, therefore, be no general rules for life. Even here they fail, and it is important to establish the indefensible extent to which their own theory is driven.

This was precisely the strategy and goal that was used and set in the courtroom by the defense on the matter of pornography and art. This very issue of pornography as a vehicle for unrestrained sensuality may well be the tip of the iceberg. Behind it moves a massive force of value-denying and morality-mocking ideas trying to clear any inhibition in Western culture's path. An implicit dehumanization is taking place here as the waters of decency are muddied in the name of secular humanism. It is, therefore, imperative for us to unpack this particular issue of art and pornography and of the purported absence of a difference between the two. As we deal with this we will address far more than the question at hand; we will expose the evil to which secular theory is inexorably drawn.

The answers the Christian gives define the difference between these two world-views because this is one of the conflicts that is tearing away at Western culture. The war of ideas rages with agendas such as these. So let us respond to that attorney.

Two immediate thoughts came to mind as I read his approach. My first thought was of Michelangelo, who, when he began to paint unclothed people, was sternly challenged by his instructor, asking him why he wanted to do this. Caught off guard for a moment, Michelangelo replied, "I want to see man as God sees man."

The instructor's wry smile was followed by his stern rejoinder, "But you are not God."

There is a world of thought in that caution that warns artists to rethink the self-aggrandizement behind their aesthetic endeavors. Art does not have a sovereignty over morality but dares to assign to itself that privilege. Sinister minds, whether or not they are artistic, cannot whitewash evil by renaming it.

My second response came as I reflected on the irrationality of what was being implied by the lawyer, who forged a false analogy by failing to differentiate some substantial points of dissimilarity between art and pornography. I borrow from C. S. Lewis's thoughts expounded in his book *The Pilgrim's Regress*. The book itself is a fascinating allegory of Lewis's spiritual pilgrimage "past the city of Claptrap and the far-off marshes of deviant thinking to the glorious reason of Christianity." His journey to God took him from the "false simplicities" of modern thought to the "complex relations" of truth. The allegory bristles with imagination and delights the mind. In this illustration we will get to the heart of the problem.

In distinction to Bunyan's *Pilgrim's Progress*, Lewis calls his account

The Pilgrim's Regress because it was written in retrospect after he had embraced the person of Christ. This new-found relationship enabled him to understand and answer more convincingly why he had rejected all else along the way. At the midpoint of his allegorical journey, he reached a crisis point of decision between the way of the world and the way of Christ. The tug of Christ had become more pronounced and the mind of Christ supremely attractive as the ideas of the world looked more and more ludicrous. But he did not know how to expose the contrast that loomed larger each day while he was still in the iron clasp of the Spirit of the Age. Lewis personified this Spirit as one who dwelt in a cavernous mountain where those who lived by his thinking were kept in bondage to his will. All of the inhabitants in his prison were in chains, existing fearfully under his Neronian stare—hollow people, bereft of a soul. "Mind-forg'd manacles," as William Blake would have called it—mental handcuffing.

In one transcending moment, John (the name by which Lewis calls himself during this pilgrimage) got a glimpse of himself through the eyes of the Spirit of the Age and saw his real enslavement. It was here that he got his clue. He noticed that he was not seen by his oppressor as a person, nor were the others in his grasp. They were just physical substances—spongy lungs, cartilaginous windpipes, chemical compounds, and so on.

The point is an important one. In a purely naturalistic universe there is nothing to transcend matter—there is no soul or spirit because that would imply the supernatural. This dehumanizing "net worth" is all that secularism has left when life is seen through the eyes of the Spirit of the Age—a discomforting but defining realization indeed in this allegorical tale.

John began to feel the full weight of this degradation. He knew he was something more than how he was perceived by his tormentor. His moment of confrontation came in an unexpected discussion with the jailer, who represented the Spirit of the Age.

Their argument began when John remarked on the nourishment and tastiness of the milk he had just consumed. The jailer had been hoping for just such a comment so he could launch his personal attack on John. He responded that John's enjoyment of the milk was positively absurd, for milk was nothing more, he said, than one of the many secretions of a cow. It was no different from any of its other secretions. This crude approach of reducing everything that was consumed to some odious comparison became the jailer's stock response—meat was just this, or eggs were nothing more than that. So went the repulsive reductionism the jailer delighted in spitting forth. The harsh deception became unbearable to John, and he seized the moment to destroy the philosophy of Spirit of the Age. The reduction of things to nothing more than this or that was the very dehumanization it had thrust upon the people by reducing them to nothing more than cartilage and tissue. "With the light of reason" dawning upon him, John exploded: "You lie! You lie because you do not know the difference between what nature has meant for nourishment, and what nature has meant for garbage!" It was the irrepressible cry of the mind against the disfiguring lie of a naturalist's universe.

At that moment in the narrative Lewis is at his best in moral theory. He portrays the bold and statuesque person of Reason, riding in on a magnificent stallion and rescuing John, applauding his answer. And as Reason latched on to John's common sense and whisked him away, "she stabbed at the heart of the Spirit of the Age with a series of piercing questions." The grim countenance of that tyrant, imprisoned by his own materialistic mind-set, could give no answer. Brain power was not sufficient to explain what the mind and the heart instinctively understood, and the demolition of the naturalist's case began. Says Lewis:

> Reason set spurs in her stallion and it leaped up on to the giant's mossy knees and galloped up his foreleg, till she plunged her sword into his

heart. Then there was a noise and crumbling like a landslide and the huge carcass settled down: and the Spirit of the Age became what he had seemed to be at first, a sprawling hummock of rock.[1]

In bringing the mind and common sense to bear upon the mindlessness and senselessness of the Spirit of the Age, John knew the blow would be fatal to naturalism. If humanity is nothing more than its lowest common denominator, the very philosophy espoused by a valueless creature is valueless. The ideas we pursue can be classified in terms of worth only if human beings have an essential glory. And if there is that essential worth in humanity we cannot reduce it to worthless usage. This begins the rejoinder from reason and common sense in response to the one who sees no difference between art and pornography. Secularism strips humanity of decency because it strips it of common sense first by denuding the mind.

Where then does that lead us? Let us not lose sight of this titanic battle in society, because it hides the heart of our struggle. Granted, in some cases there is no difference between art and pornography, not because art is the same as pornography, but because some art is nothing more than pornography masquerading as aesthetics in the name of art. But here is the point. If an artist seeks to portray the unclothed human body as art while actually bringing to that rendering his or her own lustful and vile intentions, the unworthy motive of the artist cannot be denounced by the unthinking canvas. The canvas cannot come to the artist and say, "Stop." But by contrast, the undisguised purpose of pornography is erotic and seductive. One would like to hope that the unclad individual, used as such bait in the marketing of her flesh for the sensually insatiable, would raise her hands in embarrassment, saying, "Stop, please don't do this to me." But that does not happen. Such objections are not forthcoming because when secularism has spawned its offspring, it produces a loss of a sense of shame. There is no voice within to say, "No, this is wrong. Don't do this to yourself."

This pathetic, psychological, voiceless posture where shame is excised from our cultural intercourse, leaves behind a hell of possibilities and swings wide the door to evil in any and every form. This is the unworkable pragmatism of secular thinking. All attitudes and all behavior find avenues of unbridled expression, and no one reserves the right to say, "It is not enough to say you're sorry—you ought to *feel* sorry and ashamed of what you have done." Ah! But this is too much to ask of the postmodern mind where self-congratulation is the mood engendered by irreligious social policies.

Let us be certain: It is our philosophical commitment that ends up legitimizing shamelessness that puts an individual on the road to incorrigibility. The difference between criminals who try desperately to cover their faces when they are escorted into court and those who smile remorselessly as they strut into the courtroom is civilizations apart. The ones covering their faces or shedding a tear have at least a vestige of reachability. There is at least the hint of the possibility of change, because there is a point of reference for wrong, some shared meanings between the wrongdoer and society. For any corrective in behavior or for punitive measures to be effective there must be some point of hurt or undesired feeling within the one who has done wrong. Shame or remorse or society's disapproval is powerless today to induce a desire to change, because the ideas that shape our culture make shame a hangover of an antiquated religious world-view. How then is it possible to reconcile law with liberty when both the sense of right and the sensation of wrong have been eradicated?

THE GENESIS OF SHAME

Shame is to the moral health of a society what pain is to the body. It is the sense of shame that provides an indicator to the mind. There is a powerful analogy even from the physical world of the materialist. It comes to us from the scanner theory of cancer causation.[2] This theory propounds that an incurable cancer is not ultimately caused by the cancer itself as much as by a detection system that has broken down.

According to this hypothesis, healthy cells in the body routinely become cancerous. But built into the body is a system of detection and a mechanism that comes into play to identify the cancerous cells and destroy them before they take over. It is not the cancer but the breakdown of the detection system that proves fatal.

How pitiful is the condition we have reached if we smother that sense of shame that was part of society's scanner system to detect wrongdoing and deal with it. Is it any wonder that our news journals are filled with page after page of incidents that continually shock us and are steadily bleeding decency out of life's mainstream?

The loss of shame in a society is ultimately an attack upon all of civilization. Why is that so? Put succinctly, it is this. The man who molests a child and feels a sense of shame expresses that shame because he has denuded and defaced that one person. The person who commits this same act and feels no shame in effect denudes and defaces the whole world because he is thereby telling us that our self-respect and the sacredness of physical privacy are worthless. His loss of shame is an attack upon all of humanity, because shame was given to us as a guardian, not only of ourselves, but of our fellow human being.

In *The Great Divorce* C. S. Lewis drove home this point of sensitization toward evil with riveting force as one ghost in the netherworld says to another:

> Don't you remember on earth—there were things too hot to touch with your finger but you could drink them all right? Shame is like that. If you will accept it—if you will drink the cup to the bottom—you will find it very nourishing: but try to do anything else with it and it scalds.[3]

It can be carved into the national ethos that the loss of belief in the supernatural, which secularism implies, has led to an eradication of the sense of shame, which secularism cannot deal with. That may well have been the goal in the minds of some societal engineers, but let us be sure that it produces a completely different soil than the one that brought America to its greatness. The soil of shamelessness gives root to evil in its most violent forms. The unbearable reality of secularism's consequential loss of shame is that the ones we victimize by evil can even be the ones we claim to love.

To raise a child without shame is to raise one with no immune system against evil. This was the dastardliness of the crime when the son killed the father in Dostoevsky's *The Brothers Karamozov*. This is the crime we end up witnessing when family members kill their own offspring or their parents. To remove shame is to perpetuate evil even toward the ones we love.

The catalog of crimes within families and between friends is one of the most painful and incomprehensible. The evils we foist upon children at the hands of responsible adults are not crimes born of hate. They are passions unleashed and justified by a conscience bereft of shame or remorse. Any conversation with a police officer who investigates such criminality within families reveals horror stories that stun the mind. Almost every such officer I have met has said to me that if we were to know even a fraction of all that goes on in homes behind closed doors the knowledge would be heartbreaking. Shame is meant to protect the very ones we love. But our culture has killed it. With the name of God now unhallowed and His kingdom not welcome does it make any sense to cry, "Deliver us from evil"?

THE EXODUS OF LOVE

Through secularism, this mood of a society without shame now covers the land. We may analyze the carriers and progenitors that led to this state ad nauseum, but it all ultimately points back to the first three chapters of the Book of Genesis. The big question Adam and Eve were asked was, "Has God *really* said . . . ?" When they questioned the reality of His voice and supplanted it with their own authority, they made themselves the measure of all things. No sooner had that choice been made and God's voice overridden than the feelings of fear and shame overcame them, and they tried to cover themselves.

Shortly thereafter, the Voice from Without came to them again: "Adam, where are you?" God knew the answer to that, but it was an opportunity for them to recognize their transgression and to repent of it. God in His grace provided a covering for their sin.

Just one generation later when Cain murdered his brother Abel, the Voice from Without came again: "Cain, where is your brother Abel?"

Now there was no shame, no remorse. "Am I my brother's keeper?" thundered forth the response, bereft of shame. There was no covering this time. The divine pronouncement was unequivocal. "You will be a restless wanderer on the earth."[4] The silence would now be one of apprehension, of ever looking over his shoulder.

It was Luther of old who once cried out, "Bless us, oh Lord; yea, even curse us, but please be not silent." Secularization—the silencing of the supernatural—brings about an eerie silence. And there is little consolation for Christians inside their church walls to wag their fingers at a dominant landlord who owns everything else, even the conscience of a nation. There is even less consolation for secularists who own a small container in which to carry their gasoline but have no car in which to put it. Even if one were procured, the villager still has to be taught the rules of the road. There are other drivers on the highways. That is what pluralization is all about, to which we now turn. In that mood we see how evil comes through another innocent but misunderstood idea.

Six

With Deference for Difference

WHEN OUR SON was only four years old and we moved to a different city, he raised a question of my wife that brought rounds of laughter from the whole family and even prompted a wistful thought—how nice it would be if life did provide such a sequence of colors. Driving in the car one day, right out of the blue he turned to my wife (who is from Canada) and said, "Mummy, when do we turn black?"

Caught completely off guard she said, "I don't know what you mean."

"Well," sounded the pensive, albeit innocent, childish voice, "You are white, we are beige, and Daddy is brown—when do we turn black?"

In his young mind, magnificently untainted by years of biases and indoctrinations, he saw life as a time-released kaleidoscope of colors and apparently envisioned the possibility of each of us experiencing the joys and hurts of all.

I must confess that the thought crossed my mind as to why God did not do it that way. How much more understanding of each other we would be if each of us could live for a time from within another's world. However, I strongly suspect that even if that were possible, we would create reasons with which to justify our intolerance of others. For reasons of pride of race, place, grace, or face, human beings somehow make room for hate. In fact, when much of the world's agonies are uncovered they reveal the immense capacity of humanity for rejection and an undying search to find someone, or some class, toward whom to vent its anger. In this, of all the centuries, we have caused so much hurt to one another that it has made even the most optimistic of us sober-minded about the tenuous nature of human relationships. This chapter deals with the differences with which we all live and how the Christian faith responds to the social phenomenon we call *pluralization*, the second mood of our time.

A BODY OF DIVERSITY

After millennia of human existence and decades of efforts and laws to find unity amid diversity, we still live in a highly volatile mix of world-views and values. Upon every American coin we have the inscription "E Pluribus Unum"—out of the many, one; out of diversity, unity. This was to be the melting pot, but painfully and unfortunately the analogy too often resembles a simmering cauldron, precariously close to boiling over. Political convictions are very diverse and seem increasingly anger-ridden. The rhetoric used to challenge another view has become inseparable from the rhetoric used to attack another person. Consciously or otherwise the media generate feelings of affection or disaffection about people, and intelligent debate has been sacrificed at the altar of personalities.

As if political antagonisms were not enough to fragment us, religious intolerance has also raised its countenance in settings around the world. Added to this mix is the gender conflict, which in intensity is at an all-time high and is possibly the most sensitive issue on university campuses today. But most volatile of all is the disheartening constancy with which ethnic tensions have led to crimes on a global scale. Of all the struggles we face in living with our fellow human beings, here, it was assumed for some time, progress would have been made. Yet, just as the word *multiculturalism* gained common usage and propelled social change, *ethnocentrism* made a discomforting entry. In three short decades the plaintive cry for harmony in our increasingly diverse world has been silenced, drowned out by the militant screams of isolationism under the banner of celebrating distinctives.

[There is a very thin line of difference between the legitimate pride of self-acceptance and an illegitimate self-exaltation that fosters superiority and alienation] It is in this context that our attention is drawn to the second mood of contemporary society, that of pluralization and a search for community and the evil it begets when it is misunderstood.

Very simply, pluralization is defined as the existence and availability of a number of world-views, each vying for the allegiance of individuals, with no single world-view dominant. It has been primarily in the last thirty years that the North American mind has had to make a popular appraisal of what the world believes and then respond culturally to such varying descriptions of reality. With the arrival of people like Maharishi Mahesh Yogi, for example, and the popularization of his Eastern meditation techniques, a whole new world of reflectiveness was introduced into the harried pace of the dynamic, economically driven lifestyle of the West.

The cultural revolution that began thirty years ago called for a rejection of the old and the embracing of the new. Paul Simon sang a dirge to the era that was being displaced and reviled a generation which paid homage to its neon gods. Pete Seeger castigated the materially minded who lived in "little boxes on the hillside, little boxes made of ticky-tacky, little boxes . . . all the same."[1] Carly Simon traced this spiritual journey through the alluring streets of Cambridge to the bucolic life in the country, only to conclude:

> Now you run a bookstore
> And you've taken on a wife,
> And wear patches on your elbows
> And you live an easy life.
> But are you finally satisfied?
> Is it what you were lookin' for?
> Or does it sneak up on you
> That there might be something more?[2]

But this was only a small sound bite amid the high-decibel discord of many new voices. The soul of America was tested again as pluralism became a reality in the country's decision-making process. Once again moral categories were not easy to establish, because what was anathema to one culture was a blessing to another. Pluralism became a vital force in the West because it came at a time when weariness with mainstream religion provided justification for many to dabble in other ways of thinking.

However, the change of cultural and philosophical mix took a strange twist. These new ideas that were planted in the mind were no longer just "visiting" ideas. Rather, the proponents of these ideas and the pockets of new belief systems had begun to reside in the West and, in fact, to audaciously demand not only a change in Western thinking, but privileges that the West itself would never be granted in foreign soil. By acceding to those demands, a new America was forged—spiritually unsure of itself, bereft of cultural confidence, and glorying in self-deprecation. It has become the "in thing" now to "think foreign," or radically, and the outrageous thing to affirm Western strengths, or "think conservative." This shift is not just imaginary; it is real. A journey into the past once again shows a fascinating trail.

THE SIGNS OF TENSION

In a sense, the present scene in America was prefigured at a conference on world religions held in Chicago in 1893. There, a notable and brilliant Indian religious scholar, Vivekananda, was to rattle the rafters and challenge the mind of the West with the thinking of the East as never before. As he extolled the glories of Hinduism and castigated the abuses of Christianity and Islam, the delegates to that conference were roused by his exposition and wooed by his pathos. His provocative address launched a full-scale attack on the "imperialist West," charging it with an attitude of dominance and superiority. His polemic accomplished his goal, and he may well have set the mood for all future religious interaction at the level of a world platform. Though his thoughts were strongly worded, they might have opened meaningful dialogue had he been more sensitive and had those responding been able to differentiate between fact and perception. But that was not to be. Some of his ideas and his accusations were unfortunate, and in fact, misleading. Here is what he said:

> We who come from the East have sat on the platform day after day and have been told in a patronizing way that we ought to accept Christianity because Christian nations are the most prosperous. We look about us and see England, the most prosperous Christian nation in the world, with her foot on the neck of 250,000,000 Asiatics. We look back into history and see that the prosperity of Christian Europe began with Spain. Spain's prosperity began with the invasion of Mexico. Christianity wins its prosperity by cutting the throats of its fellow men. At such a price the Hindu will not have prosperity. I have sat here today and I have heard the height of intolerance. I have heard the creeds of the Moslems applauded when today the Moslem sword is carrying destruction into India. Blood and sword are not for the Hindu, whose religion is based on the laws of love.[3]

His emotionally charged words encompassed all the elements that have come to represent Western uncertainty and self-recrimination and the deep-seated struggle with religious and ethnic pluralism. He gained a hearing by touching the raw nerve of racial tension; he intermixed his content with his own religion's affinity for science in general and evolutionary theory in particular; he lauded the appealing side of pantheistic tolerance and created a caricature of Christianity that was easy to attack. In essence, he combined all the issues that were dividing people—the unequal yoking of nations, the historical baggage of Christianity's abuses, and the readiness of uncritical minds to absorb contradictory belief systems. His thoughts and ideas were to open the doors of universities across the country, and a century later this inaccurate use of religious history and thought still prevails in religious discourse.

However, much of what he said, though clearly tendentious, in fact revealed a perception that was real and passionately held by detractors of the Christian faith and by critics of Western culture. We must understand that these notions and predispositions are precisely what make up the collision course on which we now seem to be headed. A mixture of truth and error can be deadly when combined with passion and power. The pluralization of the West, therefore, is a phenomenon worthy of serious attention in order to harness the strength of cross-cultural interaction and thwart the evil that threatens both the present and future generations.

THE FEATURES CHANGE

With most historical drifts, the factors of influence come from many directions, and the pluralism that has reconstituted America is no exception. The reshaping elements have come from at least three sides—ethnic, political, and religious. Each of these bring a strength but also present a warning that our thinking on these issues must be very clear. If the ideas and their ramifications are not properly thought through, the danger is immense.

According to census figures released in May 1992, during the 1980s the United States admitted 8.6 million immigrants. Within the context of this century, that number is more than in any other decade since 1910. These figures tell a significant tale because they represent half of the total number of immigrants worldwide. In other words, of all those involved in cross-national transplanting and relocating during the 1980s, 50 percent of them headed to America. It is impossible to ignore the attraction that this country holds for people the world over. A very interesting sub-statistic is also thought-provoking. Eleven percent of these immigrants to the United States during that period, i.e., more than three-quarters of a million people, specified their destination as Los Angeles.

I well remember speaking at a convocation on ethnic America in the early years of that decade and being both humored and informed by the comments of the opening speaker. He was much beloved by the multicultural audience, who responded to his introductory comments with roars of laughter when he quipped, "Where else but in Los Angeles can you find a fast-food outlet where a Korean is selling kosher tacos?" Indeed, pluralism is a reality, not just in food, but in our thinking. By the end of the decade, the City of Angels boasted a population in which 40 percent were foreign born and in which nearly 50 percent spoke a language at home other than English. That alone ought to have spelled caution, because language goes beyond syntax and grammar. Language frames a reality and structures the context out of which one relates. When a person from one culture complains that the statement he or she made loses something in the translation, it is not because the words are limited; it is because the experience brought and the sentiment provoked will not be the same in another language.

Ironically, the very timing of the release of these burgeoning statistics that describe a growing disparity could not have been more indicative of the unease that was lying below the surface. Just two weeks prior to this, America had experienced the most violent urban riot in its history. Fifty-one people were killed, and $750 million in property damage was inflicted[4] in Los Angeles in the anarchy that resulted from the acquittal of four white policemen charged with the assault of a black traffic offender, Rodney King. It is this mix, this low combustion point, this unease and apprehension, that prompted sociologists years ago to speak of the "Los Angelization of the West."

In other words, pluralization does not always provide a haven, and the stakes can be high when people are forced or prepared to risk everything. The romantic predispositions and sentimental notions of idealized relationships notwithstanding, such ambition and anticipation must be weighed against the harsh realities of the costs that are exacted when several world-views collide.

An ancient Indian proverb says, "Whatever you are overflowing with will spill out when you are bumped." It conjures up the picture of a village woman carrying an urn on her head filled to the brim with water or milk. Unexpectedly, some careless youth comes running errantly across her path, causing her to suddenly stop, and resulting in a spill of whatever she was carrying. The point of this proverb is that one's reactions may be a truer test of character than one's actions. Actions, though sometimes impressive, can be premeditated and designed to deceive, but *re*actions come from the overflow of the heart and are impulsive. And here it is that the melting pot shows itself to be, in reality, a boiling cauldron—in the turbulent issues that rock our communities. The well-moderated speeches of politicians and the platitudes of reformers may sound cool, calm, and promising, but the point of ignition is low in our streets and neighborhoods and makes the promised hopes tenuous.

Why is this so? The reason is the hidden assumption in pluralism that is often the same assumption as in secularism—the idea of relativism. Moral choices are assumed to be relative to the person's predisposition. It is unpopular to assert that even the melting process requires a medium in which a desirable mix can occur. In the final analysis, the perennial addition of ingredients requires something insoluble to contain it. The old problem of the universal solvent holds true—where do you store it?

POLITICS OF CULTURE

It would be a relatively easy task to manage the situation were it only a matter of balancing the numbers added to the cultural mainstream each year. This would be true in any country. But like all very critical issues the answers are not as simple as a single corrective. The ideas that are represented must be dealt with and sensibly discussed. The intermix goes far beyond just a cross-cultural issue. Let us now examine the three principal sources of pluralism today.

The lead article in the July 10, 1995, issue of *U.S. News and World Report*, was titled "Divided We Stand." From that mainly political perspective, the writers identified seven different voting mind-sets. Each of the "species" was further defined by a television character who was representative of its values. I must confess that, not desiring to spend my life in front of a television, many of these mascots were unrecognizable to me, but the assumption may be made that to most of our "educated by vision" group, this would not be a problem. The seven types of voters were: (1) the populist traditionalist, as represented by Roseanne's husband, Dan; (2) the stewards, represented by Thurston Howell; (3) the dowagers, represented by the "Golden Girls"; (4) liberal activists, represented by Murphy Brown; (5) conservative activists, represented by Alex P. Keaton; (6) ethnic conservatives, represented by Louise Jefferson/Edith Bunker; and (7) agnostics, represented by "Frasier." The writers were also careful to point out that there was a "don't know" category, but did not elucidate how the "don't know's" differed from the agnostics.

In each of these categories the political perspectives are deeply felt, and the convictions of "how to govern" are very diverse. If diversity of governance were all that divided the group it would be understandable. However, when anger is vented in disagreements, it is very disconcerting. One need only reflect on the vilification that took place when the conservative Vice-President Dan Quayle questioned the ethical implications of a Murphy Brown-type lifestyle. It was as though centuries of hatred was unleashed as a result, and the ideological clashing of swords cut deeply.

Political differences have taken such a turn because, to the pluralistically minded in a secular culture where shame has already been excised, the power to create and enforce moral relativism has been placed into the hands of government. Political power is a strange place to entrust morality because proverbially politics is not synonymous with moral uprightness. The very institution that is distrusted by most has now become the shaper of the soul. Aesop of old had innumerable stories on what lay ahead for such credulity.

RELIGION SEEKING REPRESENTATION

A further alteration in America's cultural landscape has come about with the drastic shift in religious commitment. In a subsection of his fine work *Culture Wars*, James Davison Hunter has given us a remarkable study and pointed out the changing mix here, as well. The Catholic component, for example, has played a fluctuating role in the American ethos by virtue of its numerical status. In the 1830s, 600,000 Catholics arrived in America. In the 1840s, that number rose to 1,700,000. In the 1850s, there were 2,600,000 Catholic immigrants, and hence, the shift within a century from a Protestant predominance previous to 1830 to a swiftly changing tide. In the 1790s Catholics comprised 1 percent of the total population. In the 1920s that changed to 17 percent of the population, and by the mid-1980s nearly 29 percent of the population of the United States was Catholic.[5]

The Jewish scene is quite different, moving from comprising one-tenth of 1 percent of the population in the 1830s to forming 3 percent by the 1920s. Writing in the 1950s, Will Herberg pointed out that American culture had become a roughly comparable blend of Protestant, Catholic, and Jew.[6]

This is a vitally important point to note. In spite of economic rivalries and even hostilities between these three religious groups, in spite of prejudices and several points of tension, in broad strokes there was nevertheless a biblical theism common to all on the questions of origin and destiny. God was understood as being personal, morality had a bearing on reality, and accountability to a higher law was implicit to all moral demands. Even natural law, i.e., nature's "order," was considered to be part of the revealed truth from the Creator.

But this intermix was to face a foundational struggle from a social theory coming from a new direction. As has already been described, secularism, the offspring of the Enlightenment that exalted reason, inevitably brought about not only the dethronement of God but also demanded a radical redirection away from issues of the soul to an exclusive focus on "this worldliness."

With a philosophy diametrically opposite of secularism, Islam has recently begun to make a serious impact both globally and in America. In the 1930s there was only one mosque in the United States and fewer than twenty thousand Muslims. By the late 1980s there were over six hundred mosques, and more than four million Muslims inhabited the country. This very real presence of Islam may well be a positive thing in the long run if calmness and courtesy can prevail, because for the first time in centuries of history we have the possibility of meaningful interaction with one another. The Christian will be compelled to better understand what he or she believes and to know how to defend that belief.

But what America's secular-minded social engineers need to constantly remember is that Islam defines history from a transcendent perspective with temporal application. Consequently, Islam seeks to translate the law of Allah, derived from the Koran, into the law of this land. To some in Islam's ranks that vision alone justifies all actions. Transcendent leverage is given to present upheavals and laws. This view of social theory is radically different from a secular, this-worldly perspective of life's purpose.

The attraction of Islam to the "disenfranchised" in many countries, especially in the United States, is that Islam is more than a religion; it is, in fact, a geopolitical theory. The gains Islam has made in the black community are indicative of its appeal to those dissatisfied with the establishment. The conversion of Cassius Clay into Muhammed Ali was symbolic and well represented by Ali's poetic fervor. He said something to the effect that he wanted "no pie in the sky by and by when I die, but I want my castle on the ground while I'm around." This combination of discontent and geopolitical intent have a tremendous bearing on the pluralization of American values and ideals, a situation that is equally true in Great Britain. Secularism and Islam by definition are on an ideological collision course.[7]

The influx of Eastern pantheistic religions, i.e., Hinduism, Buddhism, and Zen, introduced another dimension and further reconfigured the Western world. The more popular forms of these ideas, often called New Age teachings, are also well known and have made inroads into the business community by offering meditational techniques to increase professional performance. If a Christian were to refuse an invitation to participate in Eastern meditation on the basis of his or her own faith, the followers of the guru would smilingly counter with, "Oh, but you can do it during your lunch hour." Such is the dichotomy enjoined and the possibility offered by pluralism.

Beneath the surface congeniality, however, this diversity and these deeply felt religious distinctives bring with them a challenge of monumental proportions.

VULNERABILITY OUT OF STRENGTH

There is again one fundamental difference from the early mix of people in America, in contrast to the present drastic change. When discussing America's dream in the making with diversity as its strength, no quotation is more familiar to the student of ethnic confluence than the one by French immigrant and loyalist Michel Guillaume Jean de Crevecoeur in his essay, "What Is an American?" His statement has recently come under fire from some as being biased. While that criticism may be worthy of serious note, it is important not to bypass the reasoning behind his praise of America, for that oversight misses the logic of what de Crevecoeur said:

> He is an American who leaving behind him all his ancient prejudices and manners, receives new ones from the new mode of life he has embraced, the new government he obeys, and the new rank he holds. The American is a new man, who acts upon principles. . . . Here individuals of all races are melted into a new race of men.[8]

If this statement is descriptive of a willing predisposition when adopting a new homeland, that is, to leave behind ancient prejudices and melt into a new race, then the modern influx of world-views makes the dream very elusive. The points of tension are too many and, for most, are nonnegotiable. More is brought in today than is left behind.

These factors of culture, politics, and religion, all struggling in increasing proportions for unfettered expression, have made North America an intensely and voluntarily pluralistic society. This is not merely a changing face; it is a reconstituted mind. When demographics such as the shifting proportions of old age to youth and the increasing power of youth in the economy are factored in, the resulting changes are only further complicated. The commercialization of Christianity—where feeling has replaced thinking—has played no small part in this process, either.

In short, pluralism with all its strengths and hazards makes this tail end of the twentieth century one of enormous possibility but also one of gigantic risk. The great glory and strength of pluralism is that it compels the holder of any belief to measure its truthfulness against alternative interpretations. The great hazard of pluralism is the faulty deduction, in the name of tolerance, that all beliefs can be equally true. It is ultimately truth, not popularity or rights, that determines destiny.

It has been correctly stated that religion is the essence of culture while culture is the dress of religion. The intermix in our society today leaves one completely apprehensive as to what will become of the essence of the West. Will it be the nakedness of secularism, or will it be the garb of some belief that is at its core inimical to the fundamental beliefs that framed the West? Will our inability to get along unleash an evil with which none can live? Or can pluralism be harnessed in its strengths and minimized in its vulnerability?

SEEKING THE ETERNAL

For the Christian, before addressing the fundamental philosophical fallacy that pluralism courts, there are at least three vitally important principles that should condition every response.

First, it is imperative that the Christian learn to differentiate in his or her own beliefs between *opinion* and *conviction*. An opinion is merely a preference in a continuum of options. A person may prefer one color to another or one style to another. A conviction, on the other hand, is rooted in the conscience and cannot be changed without changing that which essentially defines the person. In a pluralistic culture, an opinion should not be given the same passion as the weight of a conviction. And every conviction held must be done so with the clear and required teaching of Scripture. Once these differences are made in a Christian's mind then a very important logical consequence follows: Every conviction that is held should be undergirded by love.

Without the undergirding of love, the possessor of any conviction becomes obnoxious, and the dogma believed becomes repulsive to the one who disagrees with it. The early church also lived in an intensely pluralistic culture in which it had to deliver an exclusivistic message, but the believers were distinguished and recognized by their love. Our Lord Himself proclaimed truth in exclusive terms, terms in which there was no compromise, but He demonstrated that truth by the embodiment of a perfect love. Being possessed of a conviction is a necessary part of following God, but doing so with love and patience are the necessary handmaidens.

Second, pluralism will ever be the reality by which societies are constituted, be they in political theory or religious conviction. The alternative—totalitarianism—is deplorable and terrifying. The danger for the Christian is not that pluralism exists on the outside; rather, it is the deadly effect of relativism that has taken hold of the Christian mind. The life of one who follows Christ must have the clear ring of truth to it rather than conveying a surrender in the name of pluralism to the relativism of the age.

Third, Christ never sought to establish His kingdom here on earth. He set His eyes determinedly on the cross, in full recognition that only there could a heart ever be broken and mended in order to live as a healer in a broken world. Yes, He engaged His counterparts in incisive dialogue, and He wept for them. Indeed, He knelt beside His own beloved city of Jerusalem and prayed with deep anguish for her. But He never, ever intimated that the city could be changed merely by a tougher legal system, as important as that might have been. He sought to change the hearts of men and women by the renewing of their minds through the work of the Holy Spirit. That kind of work is slower but more definite. That kind of power is moral and spiritual, and in the long run outdoes brute force and hate.

The words of Malcolm Muggeridge come to mind and encourage the heart that our struggles are not new and that our confidence can remain unshaken:

> The world's way of responding to intimations of decay is to engage equally in idiot hopes and idiot despair. On the one hand some new policy or discovery is confidently expected to put everything to rights: a new fuel, a new drug, détente, world government. On the other, some disaster is as confidently expected to prove our undoing. Capitalism will break down. Fuel will run out. Plutonium will lay us low. Atomic waste will kill us off. Overpopulation will suffocate us, or alternatively, a declining birth rate will put us more surely at the mercy of our enemies.
>
> In Christian terms, such hopes and fears are equally beside the point. As Christians we know that in this world we have no continuing city, that crowns roll in the dust and that every earthly kingdom must sometime flounder. We acknowledge a King men did not crown and cannot dethrone, and we are citizens of a city of God they did not build and cannot destroy. Thus, the apostle Paul wrote to the Christians in Rome, living in a society as depraved and dissolute as our own. Paul exhorted them to be steadfast, unmovable, always abounding in God's work, to concern themselves with the things that are unseen, for the things which are seen are temporal but the things which are not seen are eternal. It was in the breakdown of Rome that Christendom was born. Now in the breakdown of Christendom there are the same requirements and the same possibilities to eschew the fantasy of a disintegrating world, and seek the reality of what is not seen and eternal, the reality of Christ.[9]

To that cultural breakdown and the exposure of one fundamental danger in misunderstanding pluralism we now give our attention. This study will help in the important discovery that it is not color that informs our ideas but our ideas that color our world.

Seven

The Flickering Flame of Reason

THE ASSUMPTION that all ideas are equally true is false. Philosophically it is very easy to demonstrate that falsity. Any society, however sincere, that believes in the equality of all ideas will pave the way for the loss of good ones. What *is* true, however, is that most people are guided in life by a handful of ideas, and therefore it is all the more important that there be a way of measuring why one idea is chosen over another. This is the issue at the heart and soul of Western pluralism; on what basis have we surrendered ourselves to the ideas that govern our culture?

One of the symptoms of a society that has lost its ability to think critically is that intricate issues are dealt with in a simplistic manner. The uncritical adherence to simple platitudes uttered by the masses is proof of this and demonstrates a failure to take into consideration the complexities that lie beneath the surface of our impassioned slogans.

For example, we speak of freedom as if it were a virtue only when it is devoid of all restraint and absolute in and of itself. As cherished as that ideal may be, failure to understand the ramifications of that kind of freedom in a culturally diverse society brings tyrannies a thousand times worse. Freedom can be destroyed, not just by its retraction, but also by its abuse.

Pluralism is precisely that kind of a challenge, for beneath the simple goal of peaceful coexistence lies a web of disparate concerns. It is an ever-present temptation in free societies to latch on to one or two good concepts while failing to recognize that those ideas presuppose other indispensable conditions. Underestimating the complexities beneath our oft-quoted platitudes undermines the foundation on which the truisms stand.

In his brilliant book *Bridge on the River Kwai*, Pierre Boulle gives us a memorable account of how self-destructive a simple albeit great idea can be whose complexities are not appreciated. Told against the historic backdrop of the Second World War, Japanese-held prisoners of war were put to work to build a bridge that would link the Japanese rail system all the way to Burma and pour more firepower into that theater of warfare. Building that bridge was a vital step in ensuring Japan's military success.

The bridge could obviously be devastating to Allied efforts. Adding insult to injury, the prisoners of war ordered to carry out this project were, in effect, erecting a structure for the defeat of their own homelands. Naturally, the commander met with staunch resistance from the highest-ranking British prisoner, Colonel Nicholsen. But his resistance was for a completely different reason than one would have expected. Nicholsen agreed to organize the project but only under the Geneva Convention Pact, which demanded that officers not be forced to do manual labor. This simple but "honor-saving" insistence became the focal point of a contest of wills between the Japanese commander and the British colonel. The commander was determined to subdue Nicholsen's will in this matter, and he employed severe punitive measures to break down the British officer's stubbornness—starvation, solitary confinement, torture, and all the deprivations of personal dignity.

Finally, the Japanese commander recognized that by pursuing this personal battle of his he was running out of time to complete the bridge. At the risk of his own humiliation he granted Nicholsen his demand, with Nicholsen's guarantee that the bridge would be ready in time. Nicholsen put his genius and his fellow prisoners of war to work. He developed a passion for excellence and wanted to make this the best bridge ever built. He gave attention to every detail so that the Japanese forces could transport all of their heavy equipment with safety. In fact, Nicholsen became so obsessed with proving British engineering brilliance that he even changed the site of the bridge to make it sturdier and more easily protected from "enemy sighting."

The soldiers and officers under Nicholsen's authority were completely confounded. Why would Nicholsen want to construct an edifice of such perfection that would only enhance the enemy's capacity to destroy their homelands? They wondered if he had gone mad in his zeal for protecting a lesser idea, the dignity of officers, at the cost of a greater love, the safety of his country.

The story gains incredible intrigue as, unknown to him, a group of officers around him devised a plan to blow up the bridge just as the first Japanese train transporting its military might would pass over it. These two goals working at cross-purposes with each other occupy the last moments of the story. As Nicholsen raced against time to complete his bridge for the enemy in the name of British ingenuity and within the "nonnegotiable" proviso of the Geneva Convention, an undercover group from within the ranks was making plans to blow it up.

With the bridge completed, Nicholsen proudly marched across its expanse, flushed with pride, checking every beam while underneath the bridge the wiring was being set in place that would destroy it as the train approached. Melodramatically and predictably during this, his final inspection, Nicholsen detected some strange cables in the pillars and rushed to see what was happening. Suddenly realizing that sabotage was under way, he engaged in a hand-to-hand struggle with these "subversives" in the ranks. At the critical moment he staggered and fell wounded onto the lever that detonated the explosives and himself destroyed the bridge at the very moment the train was crossing over. His last words were somewhat intentionally ambiguous— "What have I done?"

This is a classic illustration of a man who got lost in a sublime principle in which he won a small personal battle but lost sight of the bigger war. And to add to the irony, his adversary was willing to lose a personal battle in order to win the bigger war. How fraught with danger are principles we repeat to ourselves, especially if they come in the garb of philanthropy or altruism.

Pluralism and diversity are such principles, attractive to all of us. But if they are left without other informing factors and parameters, they can serve the cause of inimical forces to destroy the very commitments that gave us the possibility of the freedom in diversity we so cherish. The evil generated by the destruction of those commitments crushes the very ones who nobly defended an uncritically pursued principle. Let us take a brief look at both the simplicity and complexity of multicultural existence to understand the ramifications.

DEFINING THE STRUGGLE

"Culture," said sociologist Daniel Bell, "is the effort to provide a coherent set of answers to the existentialist situations that confront all human beings in the passage of their lives." This simple definition is very refreshing and free from the long list of qualifiers that some scholars use in defining culture. The search is for coherence in the existentialist situations, that is, situations with which we all are confronted—from what we cherish to what we abhor, from how we live to how we die, from what is sacred to what is profane, from how we feel to how we react. Culture is the glue that holds our common values together. At first blush this may seem self-evident if we are seeking to live with each other, for we all know that there must be a shared commonality. But often at life's most painful intersections this does not happen because the points of contact between us are not casual but intense. The closer a home is to its neighbor the greater the possibility of conflict between the two.

I recall once being at a dinner for the ambassadors to the United Nations. I had already been alerted that the seating was unalterable and as fixed as the laws of the Medes and Persians. There were to be no changes because some ambassadors had come with the categorical condition that they not be placed at the same table as the representative of a nation hostile to them. As the evening progressed, I dared to ask one of the ambassadors at our table what hope he held for the United Nations. He made a very politically noncommittal statement and then said, "The good news is that we are talking to each other; the bad news is that we don't talk the same language." Somewhat puzzled, I asked, "Don't you use interpreters?" He looked even more befuddled than I was and then added, "Oh no, no, no, you don't understand. Of course we use the same language. Where we differ is in the contrary meanings we choose to assign to the same word. When I say 'peace,' I mean 'peace—no guns.' When he says 'peace'"—he pointed to another ambassador from a neighboring country, fortunately sitting tables away— "he means that I should remove my guns while he keeps his guns pointed directly at me."

This is just a small indication of the massive barrier that pluralism brings, even when the goal is reconciliation. For the Westerner, secularization may provide the steam for running the engine of culture, but in a pluralistic society the tracks are pulled up and different ones are laid down. Living under the illusion that we are safe because of assumed parameters, we only bring hazard to our journey together. At their core, cultures operate in a given situation in ways that are fundamentally opposed to each other, each culture guarding its own past prejudices and convictions.

THE LIGHTER SIDE

For those who have ever seen Indian movies, the illustration I share now will be well understood. India is the largest movie-producing nation in the world, and to grow up in India is to grow up in a culture where anything on the screen always brings a crowd. But romance on the screen was, at the time I was growing up, very typical. Since kissing was not permitted by the cultural ethos, romantic encounters routinely consisted of a "boy meets girl" scenario that ended with starry-eyed expressions, each chasing the other, generally in a treed lot while melodramatic music added to the atmosphere. It is best described as grownups playing peekaboo in a jungle. Just as the pursuer and the pursued would meet and the long-awaited moment of embrace would finally come, the scene would suddenly change, and the audience would applaud. An Indian comedian who wrote a question-and-answer column in a national film magazine was once asked, "What is the difference between love on the Western screen and love on the Indian screen?" His answer was in one word: "Trees."

In the existential questions of our lives and in the struggles of our minds, the trees that separate the worlds of culture are numerous. In fact, the same comedian sang a famous song that, translated, says, "My shoes are Japanese, my trousers are English, my hat is Russian, but my heart is Indian." Need it be added that it is the heart that beats out life's passions? Pluralism is ultimately a contest, not only of the intellect, but of the mind and heart. And sometimes those heartfelt passions can bring terror.

THE DARKER REALITY

In 1983 William J. Winslade, codirector of the UCLA program in medicine, law, and human values, and Judith Ross, lecturer in the department of psychiatry, wrote a book titled *The Insanity Plea*. In this book, seven major criminal cases were considered to show the effects of "psychologizing" criminal behavior in Western culture to the point that brutal acts of murder can be overridden by invoking cultural and psychological contingencies.

One of the cases in this compendium is called "The Kiss of Death." It gives a sad and heartrending account of the murder of a nineteen-year-old Berkeley student named Tanya Tarasoff. She was a promising student of Russian descent, born in Shanghai, with dreams of a future in America. All who knew her described her as outgoing, carefree, and flirtatious. Consistent with her personality and with no serious intentions, she befriended a young man from Asia, who was, for his part, quite enamored by her. Coming from a radically different system of values, he mistook her playful hugs and kisses on festive occasions for romance. He became obsessed by the desire to marry her and finally proposed to her. When she lightheartedly turned him down, he reacted with dismay. That bitter disappointment festered into scorn when he interpreted her flippant rejection of his proposal as a personal humiliation. To him, it was an affront to his honor and to the decency of his intent.

Gradually overcome by depression, he stepped on the path to murder. That dreadful deed accomplished, like a schizophrenic he convulsed with despair as he saw her stabbed body at his feet, dead at his own hands. Shocked and dazed, he reached for the telephone to call the police and confessed to what he had done.

Although an insanity plea is what got him off, his attorney buttressed his cause by underscoring the effect of two cultures on a collision course. As drastic and deadly as this illustration may be, the relationship may well have been fraught with misunderstanding right from the start because each gave a different meaning to the same behavior. And here is the point: If our misunderstandings are multiplied across numerous cultures and prejudices, the points of variance only increase as pluralism then exposes its sharp edges. There are no shared meanings of the past and no common mind-set—our lives have converged for economic reasons, our allegiances to the past are diverse. Suddenly people worlds apart in their values are neighbors in search of common ground.

To this one might legitimately counter that if the shared meanings of the past are an indispensable component in culture, should not the conflicts exist only in one generation and be moot in the next one? Though one might wish it were so, this is precisely where cultural roots are long and strong. Religion is just one aspect of culture. In some cultures the way one relates to society is so ingrained that centuries will not eradicate it. If the constant turmoil in the Middle East has proven anything, it is how we transfer grudges and prejudices for generations.

THE ROOTS OF DIFFERENCE

Paul Tillich, the noted liberal theologian, spoke of three kinds of cultures as they relate to religious knowledge. The names he assigned to them are distracting and the ideas seem unwieldy. But the concepts underlying those categories are very accurate. He speaks of cultures that are heteronomous, theonomous, and autonomous.

He defines a *heteronomous* culture as one where forms and laws of thinking and acting are directed by an authority outside of the individual. The authority is provided by an ecclesiastical body or a political structure. Islam and Roman Catholicism provide appropriate examples of heteronomy in religious history. In Islam, particularly in the Shiite sect, the religious figure of the Imam is given such status of interpretational authority that he reaches the level of an infallible voice. For the Shiite, the authority of the Imam or the authority of the habits and customs of their prophet Mohammed for the Sunni provides outside and "dictatorial" authority for the life of the Muslim. To that authority the Muslim must submit—that is the very meaning of the word *Islam*.

In the political arena Marxism, or any form of dictatorship, provides an example of a heteronomous culture. Here again the authority is outside the level of the mainstream of life and is imposed upon it.

Theonomous culture, on the other hand, is one where the authority from without and the intuition from within each individual life are synonymous. Hinduism provides a classic and rare example. The parameters of belief are so wide that any aberration or contradiction is seen only as either temporary or apparent. Ultimately, it is held that the roads of all beliefs will converge and there is no reason to deem one road more truthful than any other. The only wrong move, they say, would be to switch roads, or "convert," for that would imply a dichotomy of truth and error that is not essential to reality itself. The mainstream of India's culture, with all of its diversities, maintains this belief that truth is intuitive and that the moral law (Karma) determines the reincarnational cycle. This is not imposed from without. It is believed that both the circularity of life and the moral imperative are intuitive to all of humanity.

It is very difficult to meaningfully argue against such a position, because the Hindu responds that sooner or later the disagreeing individual will arrive at the higher level of knowledge and agree.[1]

Finally, there is the *autonomous* culture. Here every individual is self-determining and independent of authority. Morality imposed from without is resisted, and intuition as grounds for belief is optional. In short, autonomous cultures deny any moral authority and shrug their shoulders at intuition. The word *autos* means "self," and *nomos* means "law." North American culture and much of the West lives with autonomy at the core of its values.

To sum up Tillich's categories: Heteronomy argues for a "different" law that comes from without; theonomy argues for "God's law" that is intuitively within ("god" being defined differently by pantheism than the Christian would define God); and autonomy argues for "self-law" as the only law. The question then arises: Can an autonomous culture absorb theonomous and heteronomous cultures and still remain autonomous? The answer to that is no, not without the compromise of major assumptions.

It is this unwillingness of the West to see the fundamental differences that makes the situation so perilous. Daniel Yankelovich described a cultural revolution as that which makes a decisive break with the shared meanings of the past, particularly those that relate to the deepest questions of the purpose and nature of human life. Western culture and Eastern culture are built upon diametrically opposed foundational beliefs of what brings life meaning. And we must recognize this if we are to relate meaningfully and to understand one another. The deepest questions of life elicit opposite answers. The question is, how do we bridge them? To assume that we have common parameters on the most basic questions is to delude ourselves.

I am reminded of the humorous anecdote of a nervous flier aboard a turbulent flight. As the woman's discomfort continued, the flight attendant tried every conceivable way to ease the mind of this passenger and to assure her the plane could take an extraordinary amount of pounding and still be safe. Noticing, however, that her agitation was unabated, the attendant decided to ask for the pilot's help.

A member of the cockpit crew came into the cabin and, taking the hand of the distraught traveler, he said, "Madam, as you look outside the right window, do you see a light blinking?"

"Yes," she said nervously.

"As you look outside the left window, do you see a light blinking?"

"I do," she murmured.

"As long as we stay between those two lights," the crew member said, "we are safe."

He returned her sweaty palm to her with the reminder that each time she felt impending death she should look to the right and to the left and remind herself that the blinking lights meant they were on the right track.

Like the train that laid its own track, this assurance was an illusory one, for obviously the aircraft could plummet headlong with its lights still blinking on either side. The path pluralization provides is equally unconfirming of safety, for the lights are not a path at all but are locked into the performance of the aircraft itself. Its safety is dependent upon itself.

THE FATAL FLAW

Pluralization offers much in the way of variety, and the enrichment we bring to one another is incalculable. But when pluralism breeds a doctrine of relativism the cost has been too great. The abandonment of some necessary transcultural parameters has given way to the absence of reason in the contemplation of life's deepest questions. The end result is a cultural amalgam that will be unstable in its journey. That instability is now represented in the loss of reason. If the loss of shame was the child of secularization, the loss of reason is the child of pluralization.

This may be the key indicator to why there is such a sense of alienation in this so-called Generation X. Over half a century ago, G. K. Chesterton saw this coming.

> The new rebel is a skeptic and will not entirely trust anything. He has no loyalty; therefore, he can never be really a revolutionist. And the fact that he doubts everything really gets in his way when he wants to denounce anything. For all denunciation implies a moral doctrine of some kind and the modern revolutionist doubts not only the institution he denounces, but the doctrine by which he denounces it. Thus, he writes one book complaining that imperial oppression insults the purity of women, and then he writes another book, a novel, in which he insults it himself. He curses the Sultan because Christian girls lose their virginity, and then curses Mrs. Grundy because they keep it. As a politician he will cry out that war is a waste of life, and then as a philosopher that all life is a waste of time. A Russian pessimist will denounce a policeman for killing a peasant, and then prove by the highest philosophical principles that the peasant ought to have killed himself. A man denounces marriage as a lie and then denounces aristocratic profligates for treating

it as a lie. He calls a flag a bauble and then blames the oppressors of Poland or Ireland because they take away that bauble. The man of this school goes first to a political meeting, where he complains that savages are treated as if they were beasts. Then he takes his hat and umbrella and goes on to a scientific meeting where he proves that they practically are beasts. In short, the modern revolutionist, being an infinite skeptic, is always engaged in undermining his own mind. In his book on politics he attacks men for trampling on morality, and in his book on ethics he attacks morality for trampling on men. Therefore the modern man in revolt has become practically useless for all purposes of revolt. By rebelling against everything he has lost his right to rebel against anything.[2]

It is this undermining of our own mines that most represents the collapse of reason. The schizophrenia with which we lived just a few years ago was revealed by two front-page stories that ran at the same time. One described a professional basketball player who tragically had been diagnosed with AIDS; he conceded that he had lived a fla-grantly promiscuous lifestyle. He was, nevertheless, hailed as a hero. At the same time another renowned individual was nominated as a justice for the Supreme Court. His nightmare began when allegations were made that ten years earlier he had used some rather lewd or sexually motivated language toward a colleague, who was also a friend. This judicial nominee was publicly humiliated for these al-leged remarks that by implication deemed him unfit for the office. One, a self-defined philanderer, was hailed as a hero; the other, be-cause of unproved charges of questionable language, was labeled a villain.

Whether one should be vilified and another exalted is not the point. The point is that these opposite conditions of exaltation and humiliation did not come from a single standard. The machinations behind the scenes and the viciousness unleashed to derail the judge's nomination bred an evil even more heinous than the one it was try-ing to counter. Once again we were a culture schizophrenically star-ing into the face of our own wickedness.

THE IRRATIONAL ENTAILMENTS

The same soul-searching debate gnaws away at the conscience of the nation on the issue of abortion, pulling us apart. This contradiction was illustrated when I participated in an open-line talk program at one of America's fine and renowned universities.

The host of the program was a confessed, mix-it-up-type atheist. From the moment the telephone lines were opened, the callers vented their hostility, unblushingly using slurs and epithets. Finally, in a surprising call, a woman who had become quite outraged brought up the issue of abortion, which had not been one of the subjects under discussion even by extrapolation. Yet she raised it and charged that Christians used the issue of abortion as a smoke screen for their ultimate goal of controlling society. Her whole point of emphasis, on which she wanted a comment from me, was that the freedom to abort was her moral right. Although the main subject we had been originally discussing was the existence of God, I decided to respond to her challenge.

It was interesting, I pointed out, that on virtually every campus where I debated the issue of God's existence, some individual challenged God's goodness by pointing out all the evil in this world, especially the gratuitous evil that seems purely the result of a whim. "A plane crashes, and thirty die while twenty live . . . what sort of God is that? If God is good, why does He arbitrarily allow some to live and destine others to die?" The implication was, of course, that since God is so arbitrary in His actions He must be evil.

"My question to you, madam, is this," I said. "When you arrogate the right to yourself to choose who may live in your womb and who may die, you call it your moral right. But when God exercises the same right, you call Him evil. Can you explain that contradiction to me?" The response was nothing but anger and verbal frustration on the other end of the line. It was the torment of contradiction desperately seeking escape. We apply our beliefs selectively and judge by different standards. This is the sad result of living with flagrant contradiction that exacts a heavy toll, ultimately breeding justification of even the most irrational opinions and actions.

Think, for example, of the rationale behind the defense of abortion. The comment is often made that we do not know when life begins and therefore may abort at will. How irrational can that argument get? If my two-year-old son were missing on a friend's farm, would I go plunging a pitchfork into haystacks looking for him, because I do not know whether he is lost in a haystack? The death of reason has resulted in such loss of the sanctity of life because pluralism has bred irrationality, which is the steppingstone to the unconscionable. It is the equivalent of plunging the pitchfork into the womb because we do not know if life is there.

One of my clearest childhood memories is of being on a busy street and watching a crowd convulsing in laughter. It soon became apparent what the amusement was all about. An insane man, completely naked, was carrying on in the most senseless and irrational way. A heartless crowd had gathered and passers-by were dismounting from their bicycles to join this farce in action. The convulsive laughter continued until a policeman came and hauled the madman away to clothe him and admit him into an asylum. Even as a young person, I felt remorse at that pitiful sight, not just for the man who was insane, but for the unreasonableness of the ones enjoying his derangement.

What we laugh at and what we weep for has much to say about our rationality. One look at the current fare from our entertainment world ought to give us pause about where our reason has gone. What is more, when academia joins in and belittles reason itself and tells us that the laws of logic no longer apply to reality, then we are doubly denuded, for there is no one to rescue us.

AN INSATIABLE APPETITE

If we seek coherent answers for our culture, then we had better realize that the contradictions with which we live reveal a deep cultural incoherence. Yankelovich brilliantly points out this deadly contradiction that ushered in the eighties. He presents, among other results, the case study of a couple he calls Abby and Mark. They were a typical upper-middle-class couple, climbing the ladder of wealth and power. But with all their gaining and getting, there was an internal rupturing and bleeding. Their malady Yankelovich sums up well in a run-on sentence where "and" is the key word:

> If you feel it is imperative to fill all your needs, and if these needs are contradictory or in conflict with those of others or simply unfillable, then frustration inevitably follows. To Abby and to Mark as well, self-fulfillment means having a career *and* marriage *and* children *and* sexual freedom *and* autonomy *and* being liberal *and* having money *and* choosing non-conformity *and* insisting on social justice *and* enjoying city life *and* country living *and* simplicity *and* graciousness *and* reading *and* good friends, *and* on *and* on.[3]

Yankelovich adds:

> The individual is not truly fulfilled by becoming even more autonomous. Indeed, to move too far in this direction is to risk psychosis—the ultimate form of "autonomy."[4]

And then this postscript from him:

> The injunction that to find one's self one must lose oneself contains a truth any seeker of self-fulfillment needs to grasp.[5]

Yankelovich, of course, neither tells us how one loses oneself, nor to what. For that only Christ has the answer. But certainly we ought to see the unattainability of contradictory goals. Internal emotional estrangement and the loss of reason are connected. This is a mood that dominates in our time and is symptomatic of the mind games we play with no rules. The *ands* in Yankelovich's essay demonstrate a grim reminder that sometimes there is only an "either/or" to life's decisions, not a "both/and."

There is a reason why the law of noncontradiction is called the law of either/or. The eradication of that difference may seem to be paying deference to all sides, but in reality it signals the death of all. Shakespeare put this well:

Take but degree away, untune that string,
And hark what discord follows! Each thing meets
In mere oppugnancy. The bounded waters
Should lift their bosoms higher than the shores
And make a sop of all this solid globe;
Strength should be lord of imbecility,
And the rude son should strike his father dead;
Force should be right; or rather, right and wrong
(Between whose endless jar justice resides)
Should lose their names, and so should justice too.
Then everything includes itself in power,
Power into will, will into appetite;
And appetite, an universal wolf,
So doubly seconded with will and power,
Must make perforce an universal prey,
And last eat up himself.[6]

There must be a common string by which we tune. There must be a boundary to the waters if the whole world is to not turn soggy. There has to be a system of justice. If that does not happen strength of body will determine right and wrong. Children can strike their parents dead; our voracious appetite for power will ultimately devour ourselves. We are already seeing some of this happen. Yet there is nothing so vulgar left in our present cultural experience for which some professor cannot be found somewhere to justify it. Reason has died.

THE CONTINUING SEARCH

Can we accommodate just anything without spoiling everything? Can we believe any idea without belittling every idea? Can we enjoy love without respect for its demands? Can we claim coherence when we live with contradiction? Can we nurture the soul when we feed only the flesh? The late Richard Weaver, one-time professor of English at the University of Chicago, rightly said that if we attach more significance to feeling than to thinking, we shall soon, by a simple extension, attach more significance to wanting than to deserving.

We looked at secularism and saw how the evil it generated could end up victimizing even the ones we love. When pluralization finds no answer amid our differences to the questions of culture, evil is unleashed particularly upon those whom we do not claim to love and, indeed, end up hating. This is an important point to note. Evil toward those we identify with is born out of the first mood. Evil toward those we differ from comes by way of the second mood. Every victim of hatred and prejudice lives with that irrepressible cry within, "Deliver us from evil." To whom shall we turn? Where should we go to find answers to such pain and evil?

In God's framework we are all created equal, made in His image; yet our ideas collide, each vying for superiority over the other. Pluralization and secularization are unable to provide the philosophical base with which to pattern coherence. As we will see later, only in the created order, in recognition of God's design for people and ideas, can this conflict be resolved.

In the end, with all due deference for differences, the mind knows it cannot be indifferent to truth. Where then does one go to find truth? A secularized world and pluralized culture tell us to find it at home — and leave it there. But doing so opens the door to an evil even more seductive. That now takes us to the third mood in a disintegrating culture.

Eight

The Disoriented Self

SOMEONE HAS SAID that old age is signaled when everything you hear reminds you of something else. But that tendency comes all too early in life for it to be labeled as a sign of old age. Life affords us the privilege of making connections and finding relationships, not only with people, but also with ideas. And sometimes the most exhilarating conversation takes place when one name or one event, shared between two individuals, unlocks a storehouse of memories and a wealth of emotions. I have not been able to recall where I first heard the following story, but I do recollect it as being true.

Some years ago a person in Christian ministry from the United States happened to be visiting Romania. It was during the bitterest days of the Cold War. As he trudged slowly through a rather busy but beleaguered section of town, bundled up against the biting cold, he was aware of the somber, grim faces of the people hurriedly brushing past him. Suddenly, as if in a different world, a man walked by, his ragged, coarse coat wrapped tightly around him, a woolen scarf thrown around his neck, and a warm cap pulled tightly over his scalp, whistling a melody to his heart's content. The veteran Christian worker was caught completely by surprise, for the melody was that of a grand but not too common Christian hymn, "The Great Physician now is here, the sympathizing Jesus." Shocked to hear it on a busy Romanian street, he picked up his pace to match strides with the cheerful whistler. He was aware that he might be under observation, so, not wanting to put the Romanian at risk, he cautiously walked alongside of him and softly whistled the tune with him.

The Romanian stopped, looked, and excitedly spouted forth a barrage of words in his own tongue, his face beaming. Immediately he knew that the words meant nothing to this stranger, separated as they were by the barrier of language. As if by instinct, simultaneously they both pointed to the heavens, laid their hands on their chests, and clasped one another in an emotional embrace. Not a word was spoken, but two worlds were joined as they bade each other good-bye and went their separate ways, still whistling the same tune. In one memorable moment eternity's resources knit together two spirits, bridging two worlds, because of identical life-transforming experiences—the mending of their lives by the touch of "the Great Physician." Everything else that separated them, culture, language, political experience, and myriad other differences were set aside, for they were united by a deeper love and a transcending truth.

How stirring such an experience is, demonstrating the breadth of commonality a shared spiritual commitment brings. This deep bond born out of a relationship to Christ is possible because it reveals the most treasured pursuit of each life, and a kinship that shares the fatherhood of God. Though they had never met before, these two men knew the deepest value of the other and, on that basis, could embrace as brothers. They were linked by eternal commitments. The American visitor could not have dreamed then that the day would come when the church of Christ in Romania would play such a pivotal role in displacing a murderous and ruthless dictator. Nor could he have foreseen, by contrast, a day when the dictates of government in

America would make the naming of Christ in the public arena a risky proposition. Though Romania has proven that seventy years of a brutal atheistic regime could not eradicate spiritual hunger by relegating it to privacy, here in America we are making a fresh attempt to privatize religious belief in the hope, at least of some, to silence it.

The dramatic change in direction toward spiritual issues taken by the two contrasting ideologies of totalitarian government and democracy may be the most astonishing reversal of the twentieth century. And the confounding silence of the powers in place who leave the subject undiscussed and ignore its drastic ramifications is even more mystifying. The wildest speculator could not have predicted that religious ideas would be brought into the open for discussion in what were once Marxist countries, while in democracies the same ideas would be held, for all practical purposes, under house arrest.

A STRANGE AMPUTATION

This *privatization* of religion is the basis of the third mood in modern America, a mood that has brought a deep rift within its own culture. The concept is somewhat difficult to explain in simple terms though it is enjoined upon us all, with Christians receiving unequal victimization.

Privatization may be defined as the socially required and legally enforced separation of our private lives and our public personas; in effect, privatization mandates that issues of ultimate meaning be relegated to our private spheres. Obviously, one who disavows any transcendent meaning, or one for whom the concept of meaning itself is meaningless, is comfortably compliant with this injunction. But for the Christian, this amputation from one's deepest convictions on life's most basic questions is a mutilation of that which only makes sense when it is kept whole.

This secular handcuffing of Christianity has caused anguish-ridden confrontations in the public square. Not only are we each marching to a different drummer, finding no commonality to harmonize life, but a concerted effort is made at the same time to ensure that any public expression of the basic Christian message is silenced. The extent to which Christian conviction is muzzled reaches new and bizarre dimensions each succeeding year. One must now walk through shopping centers at Christmas and listen to bowdlerized carols from which the name of Christ has been deliberately removed so that the celebratory mood of some shoppers is not offended. Powerful voices have even demanded that the calendar be changed from the historic delineation of B.C. and A.D. because such religious intimations intrude upon our newly fashioned Western world. Is this secularization all over again? Not quite. But certainly it is its philosophical handmaiden.

While secularization has cleansed the public arena of religious ideas, privatization insists that though one may choose to believe whatever one wants to it must be kept private. This is the social phenomenon of privatization that magnanimously gives with one hand and militantly takes away with the other—and is then mystified that this benevolence is not appreciated.

This allowance for private belief supposedly distinguished democracy from totalitarianism, where one's personal belief is dictated. But in effect the same public outcome results; life's deepest quests and most cherished values are sequestered. Every thinking person knows that to imprison a sacred belief within the private realm is ultimately to fracture, if not to kill, the belief. One could no more sever belief from public expression and still live spiritually fulfilled than one could remove the heart from the body and bid the blood flow. The separation kills the life in the body. Such is the impact on privatized spirituality.

A well-known musical composition may serve to illustrate this point. Even the uninitiated into the world of great classical music have heard of Schubert's "Unfinished Symphony." But what is not common knowledge is that to the ears of the novice the composition sounds like a finished work. In fact, if Schubert had not composed it as a symphony it would not need to be called "Unfinished." A symphony by definition must have four movements, but this has only two, hence the designation, the "Unfinished Symphony." The death of the composer left the last two movements undone, and the aficionado may only now imagine how grand and climactic, how magnificent and inspiring, the completed work might have been.

This is precisely what privatization in the West has done to Christianity. The Author of creation never intended the fundamental principles of right and wrong, justice and injustice, love and hate, peace and war, wealth and poverty, sexuality and promiscuity, profit and loss, freedom and tyranny, to be aborted at midpoint or to be fluid ideas at the mercy of a changing intellectual, political, or cultural elite. Yet, ironically, this very strength of Christianity, which allows such attacks upon its truths, lends itself to such abuse, just as the very strength of democracy makes it vulnerable to destructive forces within. There are other religions that will not stand for such public abuse and will respond with unbridled violence if such suppression is demanded. The glory and the gentleness of the Christian faith makes it vulnerable to such a siege of the soul, but the greater loss is that of a culture that moves resultantly from harmony to discord. The culture that so mangles the soul will never rise to the grand crescendo written into the human heart by the Author of life.

Commitment to God most certainly has its private expression, but it implicitly directs all of life. Spiritual reality is not just a sentinel from 5:00 to 11:00 P.M. behind closed doors. Privatization with disregard for coherence forces this dichotomy. In the name of nonoffensiveness, religion is privatized and relegated to the home, while in the name of freedom all kinds of indecencies and abandonments are made public. How ironic that sexuality and nudity, which are meant to be private, are now fare for public consumption while spiritual convictions, which are meant to strengthen public polity, are now for private expression only.

This rupture has had very significant effects on the place of religion in public life and on life itself as it is lived in the West. The notion is emphatically conveyed that moral beliefs are only private preferences, and therefore all beliefs are equally valid. Also promulgated is the pathetic and false notion that what people do in private ought not in any way to impinge upon public office and empowerment. By implication, the language of religious belief has been reduced to purely emotional talk, superstitious inclination not worthy of academic recognition or acceptable in public discourse. As a result, people have been left fragmented and alienated within society and within themselves.

Secularization left society without shame and with no point of reference for decency, and pluralization left society without reason and with no point of reference for rationality. Privatization—born from the union of the other two—has left people without meaning and with no point of reference for life's coherence. The greatest victim of evil so engendered is the self. We no longer know who we are as people.

It would be impossible in a brief treatment to cover the necessary ground to fully consider all of these implications. So let us examine at least two reasons why we know that privatization is a false premise. It is easily demonstrated that private belief separated from public practice is philosophically contradictory and pragmatically unworkable. Since privatization deals with the practical thrust of secularization, rather than resorting to a formal argument I would like to present its existential impact upon leadership and upon those of us in life's mainstream. This will demonstrate the all-important counterpoint that spiritual truth brings an unbreachable connection to life, which no law on earth can ultimately sever.

A PAGE OUT OF HISTORY

We know that the premise of privatization is flawed because who we are in public *is* determined by what we have learned and cherished in private. The role of the home is ineradicably etched into the mind of every individual. We have all heard the popular saying, "The hand that rocks the cradle rules the world." History has demonstrated this to be profoundly true.

A page out of Abraham Lincoln's life brings a thrilling story to light. When Lincoln was seventeen years old, he sang a song with a tender message at his sister's wedding.

> The woman was not taken
>   From Adam's feet we see;
> So he must not abuse her
>   The meaning seems to be.
>
> The woman was not taken
>   From Adam's head, we know;
> To show she must not rule him—
>   'Tis evidently so.
>
> The woman she was taken
>   From under Adam's arm;
> So she must be protected
>   From injuries and harm.[1]

How Lincoln first came across these thoughts put to song is a strong demonstration of a life that bore the fruit of early instruction. Rather than trying to present it in my words, let me do so in the words of the great English essayist F. W. Boreham:

The quaint verses as anyone with half an eye can see, are merely Matthew Henry turned into rhyme. But what did Abraham Lincoln at sev-

enteen know of Matthew Henry? Yet one remembers an incident described by Judge Herndon—a thing that happened some years before
Abraham Lincoln's birth. A camp meeting had been in progress for several days. Religious fervor ran at fever heat. Gathered in complete
accord, the company awaited with awed intensity the falling of the ce-
lestial fire. Suddenly the camp was stirred. Something extraordinary had
happened. The kneeling multitude sprang to its feet and broke into shouts
which rang through the primeval shades. A young man who had been
absorbed in prayer, began leaping, dancing, and shouting. Simultaneously,
a young woman sprang forward, her hat falling to the ground, her hair
tumbling about her shoulders in graceful braids, her eyes fixed heaven-
wards, her lips vocal with strange, unearthly song. Her rapture increased
until, grasping the hand of the young man, they blended their voices in
ecstatic melody. These two, Thomas Lincoln and Nancy Hanks were
married a week later, and became the parents of the great president.[2]

Boreham explains that the preacher at those meetings, Peter
Cartwright, and others with him were very familiar with the biblical
commentaries of the devout English preacher Matthew Henry and
often quoted from his writings. Following the trail from Henry to
Cartwright to Hanks to Lincoln, Boreham could not resist this postscript: "It is interesting to know that at that formative stage of his
epoch-making career, the noblest of the American presidents was sitting at the feet of our English Puritan."[3]

I do not believe for a moment that Boreham has stretched his
point, because the faith of Lincoln's mother is well known, and his
love for her is proverbial. Though he was only nine years old when
she died, her last words to him were to admonish him to be faithful
to his heavenly Father.

One cannot help but wonder what would have happened to the
United States if a man of Lincoln's character had not been president
at her most painful time of internal strife as brother fought against
brother. The nation was in the grips of her most defining days. As
blood flowed and dark days beclouded the horizon, the leadership of
the land was in the hands of this great man. Who Lincoln was in

private is what made him what he was in public. We are all familiar with his famed Gettysburg Address, but we would also do well to see him with his face in his hands before God, pleading with Him to save the nation.

History is replete with the instances of leaders prostrated before God when their nation faced its most critical moments. As the spires of Russia burned under the scorching hand of Napoleon's armies the czar was on his face before God in St. Petersburg, praying for the nation. As Ferdinand Marcos's helicopter gunships hovered over a small band of eight hundred soldiers who had called for him to step down from his dictatorship, this paltry group of soldiers were having read to them the words of Psalm 91: "He who dwells in the shelter of the Most High will rest in the shadow of the Almighty." Such, indeed, are the moments that try men's souls, and if the soul of the one leading the nation has been marred, wholeness is lost at the grassroots, and malevolence sprouts from the polluted soil of culture. Evil then reigns supreme.

No one realizes this need for the strength of a nation's soul more deeply than honest, sensitive politicians. They know just how impossible is the task of leading a nation, especially at a time of crisis when passions run deep, tempers run high, and brute force is unleashed. I recall a veteran congressman telling me that Washington is the loneliest city in the world. Each day he is pulled in different directions on someone else's whim, and in each instance his deepest personal convictions are tested. Privatization may seem fair and objective at face value. But it is a mindless philosophy that assumes that one's private beliefs have nothing to do with public office. Does it make sense to entrust those who are immoral in private with the power to determine the nation's moral issues and, indeed, its destiny? One of the most dangerous and terrifying trends in America today is the disregard for character as a central necessity in a leader's credentials. The duplicitous soul of a leader can only make a nation more sophisticated in evil.

The time has come to give careful attention to whether public life and private behavior can indeed be severed with impunity. Perhaps in the short run gains in single issues may be made, but in the long stretch this thinking will destroy the soul of the culture. If those who are empowered with public trust impeach their own character in private, it *does* matter, and it ought to matter. One can no more reconcile immorality in private with a call to public integrity than one can reconcile being a racist in private with being unprejudiced in public.

WHEN LIFE DOES NOT CONNECT

Of all the scandals that feed the public appetite, the one most delightedly pounced upon by some in the media is the scandal of a minister who has betrayed his trust. A politician may lead a double life; a lawyer may shamelessly abuse the legal process; a professor of ethics may lead the most unethical life; a doctor can make killing his or her profession. But when a minister crosses over the line of propriety even slightly, the relativists mercilessly pour down the anger of an absolutist's judgment.

But if religion *is* only a private matter, why must it invade the public office of the preacher? The charge of hypocrisy is the unintended compliment that vice pays to virtue. Even the defender of privatization knows that the essence of life cannot be conveniently portioned out to some particularities of living; it must apply to all of existence, whether one is a politician or a preacher.

Many years ago Arthur Miller wrote a play called "The Death of a Salesman." The whole plot was undisguisedly intended to reveal America's cultural reality behind the drama. It was the story of a man named Willy Loman, whose whole life was a masquerade. He feigned success in business, pretended faithfulness to his wife, and crafted an image of himself before his children as a man who had all the wealth and contacts that were needed to bring every material dream within their reach. But the charade came to a sudden stop when his son, Biff, discovered the private failure and infidelities of his father's life. In bitter disappointment he agonized over the lies on which his father's entire life was built. Finally, on a fateful night when Willy Loman could take the discovery of his deceit-ridden life no more, he stormed into his car and drove recklessly into a suicidal collision, graphically portraying the reality of his own inner self-destruction. The postscript tearfully muttered by Biff said it all: "Dad did not ever know who he really was."

That is the disintegration of a double life. It breeds a schizophrenia. No one applauds when he or she has been victimized by someone else's duplicity. In this implicit condemnation lies the first point of consideration for all of us immersed in Western culture. Does Western culture know anymore what it is at its core? Do we as individuals know who we are? We all hunger for meaning and judge other lives according to their coherence. Where there is no coherence, there is no meaning. We look for coherence between law and life. We look for coherence between word and deed. We look for coherence between promises and fulfillments. We look for coherence between love and trust. In short, there is a longing to find a connectedness in life.

Cultures seek coherent answers within themselves because without coherence in community there is evil in the home and on the streets. And there is no coherence in our communities because there is no coherence in our individual lives. We cannot put into living what we do not have in life. We cannot give to others what we do not have ourselves or know where to find. In denying this generation the viability and the reasonableness of the Christian faith we have tossed away the only resource we had. We now find ourselves with nothing of the spirit to offer, only the material. That spiritual hunger must be fed or our culture will slide deeper and deeper into concoctions of evil that no civilization ever thought possible.

THE POSTSCRIPT OF THE CENTURY

As we close this section let us see how far we have traveled. Secularization led us to a loss of shame, pluralization to a loss of reason, and privatization to a loss of meaning. We noted that when secularization has bred its loss of shame it will generate evil even against those we love. Pluralization in turn has given birth to the loss of reason, generating evil toward those whom we choose to hate. Privatization kills meaning and gives rise to evil against ourselves because the alienation within mutilates the soul. No event in recent memory better encapsulates this threefold evil with which we now live than the trial of the football icon O. J. Simpson, charged with the murder of his estranged wife, one whom he claimed to love. The emotionally laden trial that gave opportunity for every trick in the book ultimately led to his acquittal. He was found not guilty by the introduction of ideas that fostered hate in our ethnically diverse culture.

But the ultimate irrationality has to be the statement made by one of his attorneys, Robert Shapiro, in his interview with television talk-show host Larry King. When Shapiro was asked by King what he personally felt about his client's guilt or innocence, he answered, "It does not matter what I think. . . . What I believe is something that really is of no importance, and I will tell you why. That's a moral judgment. And I can't make moral judgments. I can make professional judgments."[4]

Does Shapiro need to be told that the decision to make only a professional judgment rather than a moral judgment is itself a moral judgment? One must wonder whether such heartless cruelty would pass off as magnanimity if he sat where the parents of Nicole Brown Simpson sat or if it were his own son or daughter who had been murdered. Ah! But privatization has done its work in his mind. He lives under the illusion that his disconnected belief is a medal of professional excellence, failing to realize the conscience-destroying lie to which he has sold himself.

Let us take careful note. Evil does not come only in the garb of a masked murderer. In its most cunning and destructive form, it comes as an idea dressed in sophisticated attire, rationalized by these prophets of the wind. Nothing is more perverse than the idea that where murder is concerned truth and morality do not matter. But privatization reared its lying countenance in the philosophy espoused by the defense in the trial of the century. The trial may have been more than that. It is the prime example in this century of a culture that has killed shame, reason, and meaning. The evil begotten by these losses has victimized the ones we love, the ones we hate, and ultimately ourselves.

The last expression of Prime Minister Konoye of Japan, who committed suicide after his role in the Second World War, is a fitting reminder. On his night table was Oscar Wilde's *De Profundis*. The words he had underlined read, "As terrible as it was what I had done to others, nothing was more terrible than what I had done to myself."

The cultural revolution began in the sixties, and the children of that generation are now crying out for help and for answers. Who will deliver them from evil? The revolutionaries of the sixties told us then in their art that their private lives were eroding. One has only to read the lyrics of the culture in revolt to hear what they were saying. It was in the sixties that Justin Hayward and the Moody Blues sang:

> Why do we never get an answer
>   when we're knocking at the door
>   with a thousand million questions
>   about hate and death and war?
>
> 'Cause when we stop and look around us
>   there is nothing that we need
>   in a world of persecution
>   that is whirling in its greed.

> Why do we never get an answer
>   when we're knocking on the door?

With perceptive power the chorus states the innermost quest:

> I'm looking for someone to change my life.
> I'm looking for a miracle in my life.[5]

Like Oscar Wilde, that generation found it easier to live in its art. Those of this generation have carried that alienation one step beyond. They even find it difficult to live in their art. The art of this generation has reached hideous proportions of violence and hate that are then transferred into life itself. Even within the artistic world voices are crying, "Stop!" Can we hear their cry for deliverance?

No one admits to this alienation more candidly than our young. Some years ago, a pastor handed me a piece of paper on which was written a poem. He had just returned from visiting a troubled teenager who had attended some meetings his church had hosted. Arriving at the young man's home the pastor had discovered that the teenager had committed suicide and left this note behind for the pastor to read:

> Lost in a world of darkness
>   without a guiding light,
> Seeking a friend to help
>   my struggling, failing plight.
> Now all of you good people
>   just go on passing by,
> Leaving me with nothing
>   but this lonely will to die.
>
> Somewhere in this lonely world
>   of sorrow and of woe
> There's a place for me to hide,
>   but where I do not know;

For no matter where I go
  I never will escape
The devil's reaching, clutching hands,
  or the drink of fermented grape.

So out of my grief and anguish
  Perhaps some wandering boy will see,
Long after I have left this world,
  And build his own life, strong and good and free.

The quest to escape from reality has revealed that there is no place to hide. The journey of our culture has now reached its destination, a destination it never intended. A society without a point of reference for shame, reason, and meaning has very little to offer to a generation in search of *strength* with which to live, *goodness* by which to live, and *freedom* in which to live. These were the very failures that felled the Greco-Roman world.

Western culture now faces the same possibilities. We have made a decisive break with the past and have changed the soil of culture which nourished the seeds of progress. That soil is now being reconstituted, and one of the principle features of the change is the removal of boundary lines between the sacred and the profane. When that happens we court an even greater danger. Any time a decisive break is made with the past the ramifications are profoundly serious.

But the question arises, do we turn the keys of the kingdom over to religious authorities then? The Bible has much to say about changing the rules of culture in midstream and about the peril of religion that has no truth. The Hebrew world more specifically addressed the questions of national survival in transcendent terms and came to some shocking conclusions. Therefore, let us bend our ears to what the Bible has to say about culture and meaning. The Scriptures resound with lessons from history for a nation's character and for personal coherence. The truths from these voices of the past are fascinating.

Part 2

The Voices of the Past

Nine

Establishing Boundaries

THE ONLY THING more startling than a tap on the shoulder in the dark is a voice that shatters the eerie silence. And if that voice happens to be of someone who is dead, then the jolt is even more terrifying. Just such an ominous encounter was narrated to me at a home I was visiting. Understandably, it had an unnerving effect upon the one who had experienced it.

I had been invited for dinner during a conference at which I was speaking, and although he was cordial when I arrived, my host seemed notably uneasy in my presence. The conversation throughout the meal was noticeably strained, and I was quite aware of the frequent, piercing glances in my direction. After dinner, he asked if we could stroll in his backyard and talk awhile. And minutes into our conversation alone, the mystery unraveled.

While still attending college his son had been tragically killed in a car accident. "For a long time I was not able to get over my son's death," he said. "There had been many things going on in his mind that I wished we had been able to talk about. I agonized for months over the opportunities forever lost."

One day, his story continued, as he was driving on a business trip he decided to play some of his son's favorite music on tape, hoping somehow to reach back into his son's life. In what had to be a shock to him, suddenly, in the middle of the tape, his son's voice spoke as clearly as if he were sitting in the back seat of the car. The grieving father was caught completely by surprise.

The voice, of course, was on the tape itself. As the father pieced it together he discovered that a few weeks before the fatal accident, his son had made a serious commitment to Christ during some meetings at his college at which I had the privilege of speaking. So deep an impact had been made in his heart that he had returned home and recorded on tape what this commitment meant to him. It was an expression of his spiritual journey, and the mention of my name on that recording had since prompted the father to extend his dinner invitation. First, he wanted to say thank you for the role God had given me in the life of his son whom I did not even know, and second, he wanted me to know how therapeutic it had been for him to hear this voice that had passed from his life. How consoling a voice can be, especially if it is a voice we long to hear, speaking of things so profound and personal.

But there is only one voice that has that capacity to speak on matters of ultimate reality, and that is the voice of God. The Bible reminds us that God has spoken to us in numerous ways. Not only has He spoken in the written Word and in the consummate expression of His own Son, but also in the steady unfolding of the drama of history. In fact, His voice is also heard in periods that seem to be silent or in ways that seem unpretentious. We mistakenly limit God's involvement in our lives to the spectacular or the sudden. In the coinage of current aphorisms, we have ascribed only the destructive (such as hurricanes, earthquakes, and tornadoes) to "acts of God" and have missed the gracious voice that has beckoned humanity since the days of our creation. It may well be that His care and keeping are most powerfully demonstrated during those times in the life of an individual or nation when everything seems to be ordinary.

The avenue upon which we will focus now as we give ear to the voices of the past is the arena of history through which He has spoken with such inescapable force. How we read and understand history sets the parameters by which we glean the lessons it so repeatedly offers. For this reason some of the brightest minds and most influential thinkers in every century have sought to define what history is all about. In so doing they offer a key to unlock the past and shape the future, for after all, the present is the conduit that transforms the future into the past. As we probe into the past we will get a glimpse of evil's long reach and of God's shaping of the soul even through it.

THE IMPORTANCE ESTABLISHED

Karl Marx defined history in terms of economic power and its distribution between the owner and the worker. The philosopher Hegel, on the other hand, said that to lay hold of the interpretive key to history one needed to grasp not the blend of economic power as much as the interplay between the ideas that are woven through the historical process. To him, each principal idea spawns its opposite, and in the synthesizing of these opposites the historical drift finds its direction. Philosophies of history abound, and our present century has seen both the enrichment and the cost-exacting ramifications of how it is defined.

There have been others, of course, varying from the profound to the cynical, who have had their say on the subject. In the genre of the most maverick pronouncement, Henry Ford's oft-quoted quip, "History is bunk," battles for the lead. But far more radical is the statement, unfortunately more reflective of contemporary attitudes, "The past does not affect me; rather, I affect the past."

Amid the verbiage of conflicting theories, the warning words of the Romantic poet Samuel Taylor Coleridge stand out with common sense and have a ring of truth, unimpeachable even by the cynic: "If men could learn from history, what lessons it might teach us! But passion and party blind our eyes, and the light which experience gives is a lantern on the stern which shines only on the waves behind us."[1] This over-the-shoulder look at the stern lights the path we have already traversed and instructs us in some of the most important lessons so that we might avoid repeating the mistakes.

Something of cardinal importance must be added lest we reduce the world of events and biographies to an impersonal tale of one inexorable sequence of cause and effect. Behind this theater of reality is a God who is not only involved in the macrocosmic move of people, powers, and ideas but is intensely involved in each and every individual life. That is why giving ear to the voices of the past is not just a theoretical pursuit. G. K. Chesterton astutely observed, "The whole difference between construction and creation is exactly this: that a thing constructed can only be loved after it is constructed, but a thing created is loved before it exists."[2]

If history is seen as a construct of the human mind, then it is ours to love or to hate or even to ignore. But if it is seen as the arena of the Creator's self-disclosure and His love for His creation, then we can be absolutely sure of His purpose and goodwill as He works in and through His creation, indeed, a creation He loved before it even came to be. By doing so we may see the underlying truth that in the final analysis history is "His story." If we miss His story, evil will ever remain a mystery and good will ever remain at the mercy of cultural drift.

This portion of our study will take us into another time and place in history, both to look at our lives from His perspective and to gain a glimpse of what it is that God has tried to communicate repeatedly and pleadingly to preserve the purpose of our being. Only in understanding the Author of life can we cling to that which is good and be delivered from that which is evil. There is no better place to look than in the record of His story.

History understood this way is the arena in which God unfolds His truth, with the hearts of men and women as the locus in which He attempts His work. This is the fundamental difference in the definition of history that separates a secular view from a spiritual one. To the rugged materialist we just happen to be here, clothed apes, a blip on the radar screen of time, a cosmic accident. But to the Christian our existence is by the designed will of our heavenly Father who is ever in control of the universal scene. Each of us is here at this specific time within the compass of His sovereign will.

Admittedly, this is also one of the most tested beliefs for the Christian, for if we were to pause long enough to think of all the tragedies and atrocities of a single day, how easy would it be to cast all our care upon Him and know that He is in charge? Yet it is that consolation of His love for this world that enables us to see the bigger picture and not be brainwashed by isolated sound bites. That is why the role of history is so important to understand.

The cities of mankind tell a fascinating story of the reach of this God and of the resistance of the human will to Him, of the longing in the heart of God for our well-being, and of the schemes of the human heart that spell destruction. Today, if one were to travel through some of the historic cities that once displayed such splendor, the piles of rubble would speak from the past. God intended it to be so. These piles of rubble call to mind a scene from Jesus' life as He entered the city of Jerusalem from the Mount of Olives, riding on a colt, while the people irresistibly cried out to Him with shouts of praise. The annoyed Pharisees called on Jesus to order them to be silent, but Jesus replied that if they were to keep silent the very stones would cry out. The context in which He spoke these words is a worthy reminder. He warned them, first of all, to be ready for the spectacle of desecrated sanctuaries and demolished buildings that would posthumously tell the tale of their humiliation at the hands of an enemy. But He went on to underscore that the reason for this forth-coming debacle was their inability to recognize "the time of their visitation."

If the voice of God is unrecognized in its timely utterance, timeless reminders carved in stone will remain, haunting generations to come. But also implicit in Jesus' sobering reminder was the possibility of a brighter tomorrow for a nation that had "ears to hear" and would heed His call. To them would ensue a greater consolation, the promise of the recovery of righteousness and of peace—those deathless handmaidens of godliness. Such consolation is greater than the voice of one on a tape that breaks the silence from the backseat of a car. For when God speaks and beckons, the eternal has intersected with the moment, not merely to explain the past, but to instill an anticipation for the future as it is guided by the comforting hand of the One who holds it.

Let us therefore take a walk through the galleries of the past that not only show us the hall of fame but also the hall of shame. The stones and the personalities will tell us the story with buttressing eloquence. These galleries will present us with both script and deed, with the dominant role of leadership and the gullibility of the people, with the national choices made and the resultant drift of history, and with the failings of political power and the seduction of religious power. Through it all we may catch a glimpse of the strong feet of the "Hound of Heaven" pursuing the swift feet of human resistance.

The picture unfolds with clarity, and one can be overcome by the story His imprints tell. The challenge before us in such a journey will be to thwart the constant temptation to cynicism, a cynicism that leads one to wonder if the human mind is incorrigibly plagued by the belligerence of an unteachable spirit. But we will thrill to discover that just as hope may begin to fade, there will come some incredible surprises to remind the incurable pessimist that His story has not only its grim reminders, but its climactic interventions, too.

THE STONES THAT SPEAK

Percy Bysshe Shelley penned a memorable poem called "Ozymandias":

> I met a traveler from an antique land
> Who said: Two vast and trunkless legs of stone
> Stand in the desert . . . Near them on the sand,
> Half sunk, a shattered visage lies, whose frown,
> And wrinkled lip, and sneer of cold command,
> Tell that the sculptor well those passions read
> Which yet survive, stamped on these lifeless things,
> The hand that mocked them, and the heart that fed:
> And on the pedestal these words appear:
> "My name is Ozymandias, king of kings:
> Look on my works, ye Mighty, and despair!"
> Nothing beside remains. Round the decay
> Of that colossal wreck, boundless and bare
> The lone and level sands stretch far away.[3]

No part of the world offers more to the archaeologist's spade than the Middle East. Whether it be the crestfallen countenance of an ancient monarch or the faint markings upon a sacred altar in a buried commune, the wealth of information is shoveled out in spadefuls, delighting the mind as a banquet for the hungry. For our purposes, I would like to look at two very influential leaders in the Old Testament and focus on their times, their choices, and their legacies. I have deliberately chosen to focus on these periods because their times, like ours, experienced radical shifts—sometimes soaring with spiritual exuberance and at other times plummeting with reckless indulgence. The lessons of failure and success are often writ large.

The span of time this covers is the seventh century before Christ. Within this century the extremes to which the nation of Judah swung were so radical that had anyone fallen asleep between the reigns of Hezekiah and Josiah they would have assumed that the nation was basking in a century-old high noon of spiritual glory. But the reality is that the hiatus of over half a century between these two reigns brought Judah to her darkest days, days of benighted spirits and self-inflicted wounds that were mortal without being immediate. Those wounds are the most insidious and ultimately destructive, because continued survival lulls the leadership into a false security that disregards the slow bleed.

During this period the people were led by one of the most radical and destructive of all monarchs, Manasseh. That this one king, sandwiched between two of the most historic reformations in Judah, could undo during his single reign all the good that had been accomplished and would be accomplished, is a potent reminder that *any nation at any time—however spiritually alive—is always potentially only a generation away from paganism and mind-defying evil.* One can never sit back on past successes and assume a sustained strength for the future. Every generation must win its own victory.

> Once to every man and nation
> Comes the moment to decide,
> In the strife of truth with falsehood,
> For the good or evil side;
> Some great cause, God's new Messiah,
> Offering each the bloom or blight,
> And the choice goes by forever
> 'Twixt that darkness and that light.[4]

To every generation there comes that defining moment, and if it is squandered, the chain of events is long and painful. This is Western culture's hour of decision.

Ten

Pulling Down the Fences

GERMAN THEOLOGIAN Emil Brunner made the curious suggestion that Adolf Hitler should be posthumously given an honorary
doctor of theology degree because he awakened Europe to her Christian heritage by showing her what the world would be like without
Christianity. Brunner's sarcastic pronouncement would apply in the
same measure to the individual who now draws our attention, for
through him we shall see the hell that is unleashed when spiritual
truths are renounced.

With the death of Hezekiah a new and devastating day dawned
upon Judah as the leadership abandoned God and set the tone for the
people to frolic in unfettered restraint. Although on the surface the
nation mourned the loss of their great king Hezekiah, their periodic
invocation of his name and his legacy was primarily a charade, for
very quickly and drastically the spiritual climate was set back by a
generation. That reversal was brought about by the single-handed
determination of Manasseh, the son of Hezekiah. Old Testament

writers and commentators are united in describing this as one of the darkest periods in Judah's history.

If there is one word that comes close to summarizing the effects of Manasseh's reign, which tragically was also the longest one in Judah, it would be *pitiful*, for by the time he was through both he and those who had become his victims were to be pitied. They knew they were on a path to complete destruction, and though Manasseh himself belatedly recognized the evil he had wrought and tried desperately to stop the degenerative process he had started, he found out that it is easier to destroy a nation than to rebuild it. Leading a people into evil has always been an easier process than shaping a people for goodness.

John Adams, the second president of the United States and a principal negotiator to end the American War of Independence, said, "Facts are stubborn things; and whatever may be our wishes, our inclinations, or the dictates of our passions, they cannot alter the state of facts and evidence."[1]

The facts of Manasseh's reign leave us puzzled. Yet similar bents toward unmitigated evil have been relentlessly and stubbornly repeated in history, with punishing force. Malcolm Muggeridge's cynical comment, "All new news is old news happening to new people,"[2] is perennially true.

Manasseh made three specifically defined decisions that altered Judah's course and drove her to the same tragic fate that had already overtaken the Northern Kingdom. The first and most radical choice he made was to lead a reaction against his father's spiritual reforms. Manasseh was very young when he took the reigns of government, and his childish vulnerability merits our sympathy. Old Testament scholar Alfred Edersheim has described the hazards of juvenile limitation when thrust into extraordinary power, "before thought could have tempered willfulness, or experience set bounds to impulse."[3]

But the policies Manasseh pursued and the choices he made were carried out not only in the seedling years of his adolescence; they were also wantonly made in the full flower of manhood. He was consumed with a passion to break the hold of God's law upon the people. Chesterton has said that there are many angles at which you can fall, but only one angle at which you can stand straight; Manasseh was going to test all the angles.

In four painfully blunt verses, the Scriptures tell us the course he charted:

> He did evil in the eyes of the LORD, following the detestable practices of the nations the LORD had driven out before the Israelites. He rebuilt the high places his father Hezekiah had destroyed; he also erected altars to Baal and made an Asherah pole, as Ahab king of Israel had done. He bowed down to all the starry hosts and worshiped them. He built altars in the temple of the LORD of which the LORD had said, "In Jerusalem I will put my Name." In both courts of the temple of the LORD, he built altars to all the starry hosts. He sacrificed his own son in the fire, practiced sorcery and divination, and consulted mediums and spiritists. He did much evil in the eyes of the LORD provoking him to anger. (2 Kings 21:2–6)

Leading the reaction against his father's reformation, Manasseh set a personal example. It has been rightly said that before any fence is removed, one should always pause long enough to find out why it was placed there in the first place. The moral law God gave to Moses at Mount Sinai was just that. It not only revealed the nature of God and His purpose for His creation, it also served as a boundary line for the people, a line that could not be crossed with impunity.

There is no creative impulse or end result in life that provides for limitless possibilities without some parameters. In the fragile path of living, where relationships intersect and passions collide, God in His wisdom has provided fences, walls, and boundaries for our well-being, that we might not stray into terrain that destroys the very essence for which we were made. And it is these fences and walls that are coming down today with thundering force.

The social libertarian may find great ecstasy in the sound of their falling, but it may well be the very death knell of the one for whose protection the barriers were built. One of the most aberrant breeds in the American political scene these days is the one who gleefully describes himself or herself as a fiscal conservative but a social liberal. That is just another way of saying that people must live within their means financially, but can die beyond their means socially.

TRACING THE MOMENT OF CHANGE

In 1993, *Forbes* commemorated its seventy-fifth anniversary by asking eleven distinguished writers and thinkers around the world to contribute an article addressing the befuddling contradiction of the West, which, although it has so much materially is nevertheless a place where millions live lives of quiet desperation. The distinguished writers included Nobel laureates like Saul Bellow, prolific novelists like John Updike, and others of stellar credentials. Of all the wisdom presented in their preachments, the most insightful analysis may have been offered by journalist Peggy Noonan. In her article, alluringly titled "You'd Cry Too If It Happened to You," she presents this powerful illustration:

> We have all had a moment when all of a sudden we looked around and thought: The world is changing, I am seeing it change. This is for me the moment when the new America began! I was at a graduation ceremony at a public high school in New Jersey. It was 1971 or 1972. One by one a stream of black robed students walked across the stage and received their diplomas. And a pretty young girl with red hair, big under her graduation gown, walked up to receive hers. The auditorium stood and applauded. I looked at my sister. "She's going to have a baby."
>
> The girl was eight months pregnant and had the courage to go through with her pregnancy and take her finals and finish school despite society's disapproval.
>
> But society wasn't disapproving. It was applauding. Applause is a right and generous response for a young girl with grit and heart. And yet in the sound of that applause I heard a wall falling, a thousand year wall, a

wall of sanctions that said: We as a society do not approve of teenaged unwed motherhood because it is not good for the child, not good for the mother and not good for us.

The old America had a delicate sense of the difference between the general ("We disapprove") and the particular ("Let's go help her"). We had the moral self-confidence to sustain the paradox, to sustain the distance between "official" disapproval and "unofficial" succor. The old America would not have applauded the girl in the big graduation gown, but some of its individuals would have helped her not only materially, but with some measure of emotional support. We don't do that so much anymore. For all our tolerance and talk we don't show much love to what used to be called "girls in trouble." As we've gotten more open-minded we've gotten more closed-hearted.

Message to society: What you applaud, you encourage. And: Watch out what you celebrate.[4]

Peggy Noonan dealt with a harsh reality in a gentle way and warned of the delicate balance that is needed in many indelicate issues. But this very balance is shaken when fences are removed because straying becomes impossible when there is no line to differentiate between the safe and the perilous. In an unbelievable and shocking turn of events we have moved from speaking out against certain moral choices to being pressured by political enforcement and the so-called tolerant cultural elite not only to accept what was once disapproved of, but to celebrate it. Allowance for people to determine their own moral destinies has been supplanted by the demand that even that which may be repugnant or offensive to one's moral sensitivities must be acclaimed and glorified.

New experiments are made in education and entertainment that endanger the lives of impressionable children, and any voice of concern that is raised is promptly dismissed as reactionary. How many riots and suicides and broken lives is it going to take before we will give up this illusion that we can enter any zone of imagination and feed any image or idea into young minds, trusting them to their own good judgment in their selections?

Os Guinness said it best: "'Just say no' has become America's most urgent slogan when 'Why not?' has become America's most publicly unanswerable question."[5] It does not require a sophisticated moral sense to predict the outcome whenever a society pretends there are no fences. Common sense alone alerts us to the dangers.

The repudiation of the God worshiped by one's parents is a daring step and ought to be thought through carefully, because the family's worship is the scaffolding of the morality the children espouse; it helps them, with that priority, to structure their lives. This is not by any means to state that all belief, right or wrong, must be retained from generation to generation. No. It is possible that a world of error can be transmitted uncritically across the ages. But rather, this is only to affirm that whenever such a fundamental change is made, it ought to be sober-mindedly taken in full recognition of what is being uprooted and of what is being put in its place.

The terrifying reality of our current social scene with its unprecedented violence, ravaging drug addiction, and the painful specter of AIDS, is that we ought to at least pause long enough to ask whether the repudiations we have made in the past generation coupled with the current celebrating of a boundaryless existence have a direct bearing on the present tragedies.

Every now and then, especially when new crime statistics are released or when electioneering rhetoric heats up or some horrible story of a mangled life hits the press, speeches pour forth urging us to teach our children moral principles again. Few indicators of the paucity of our moral resources are more mind-staggering than a recent bestseller that was nothing more than a compilation of old stories of moral rectitude. The book sold on a massive scale, beyond the publisher's greatest expectations, with purchasers lining up at the cash register like starving peasants queuing up for bread in a famine-stricken country. That response does instill some hope, but it is going to take more than that. Just to call people back to morality, without saying why they should be moral or what morality is at its core is only another form of pragmatism. We know the fences have fallen, and we see marauding bands invading terrain that does not belong to them, and once again the cry goes out, "Deliver us from evil."

THE DEADLY DESTRUCTION

The second step Manasseh took was predictable. When any belief is expelled, one is not left with a position of neutrality. Any time a world-view is evicted, it will be replaced by another. Manasseh's next move was to accelerate the development of heathenism, and here he led the way in the most heinous practice of all—child sacrifice.

Today, to walk down into the Valley of Hinnom outside of Jerusalem brings a surge of emotion when the description is read of what took place there. Biblical scholar Cunningham Geikie describes Manasseh's dastardly practice:

> The hideous image of Moloch, the god of the Ammonites, once more rose in the valley of Hinnom, and Manasseh himself led the way in consecrating his own children, not to Jehovah, but to the grisly idol, or as the phrase ran, making him pass through the fire to the god; as if the flames, burning away the earthly impure body, let the freed soul pass through them, cleansed from all taint of earth, to unite with the godhead. . . . Human sacrifice became common at the "high places of Tophet" in the valley of Hinnom; the stately central mound, on which the idol towered aloft, rising deep and large in the midst.
>
> Night time seems to have been the special time for these awful immolations. The yells of the children bound to the altars, or rolling into the fire from the brazen arms of the idol; the shouts and hymns of the frantic crowd; and the wild tumult of drums and shrill instruments, by which the cries of the victims were sought to be drowned, rose in discordance over the city; forming, with the whole scene, visible from the walls by the glow of the furnaces and flames, such an ideal of transcendent horror, that the name of the valley became, and still continues, in the form of Gehenna, the usual word for hell.[6]

One can only imagine what all this meant to the destruction of the people's mind-set. When the king himself led the way and the sounds of burning infants were repeatedly heard echoing in the valley, it is little wonder that they called the location "hell."

Picture the scene of this unbelievable time in history. A long procession led by the king and his bodyguard followed by the thronging masses makes its way to the Valley of Hinnom. Filling the last ranks were parents holding tiny little children who were completely unaware of the fate that awaited them minutes away. In the affectionate embrace of their mothers they were oblivious to the agony through which they would be put by these same arms as they would be rolled into the flames from the arms of the idol. Think of young pregnant women watching this wondering, *Is this what I am carrying my child for?* Think of the young teenagers observing this, hearing the screams of their brothers and sisters and thinking, *Is this what life is about?* How incredible that such a scorching form of paganism could, at the whim and power of a leader who pulled out the fences of decency, replace the nobility of a righteous people.

Removing the good never stops with just that step. Defiance of that sort is not a momentary outburst on a single issue. Rebellion that sees no sanctity in life's essence is a constant state of mind bespeaking a heart that will never be satisfied. Just as a blackmailer can never have enough, so also a rebellious heart will never feel that it has enough autonomy. Leadership that caters to the rebellious will find in them an insatiable demand for more. Thus, in Manasseh's hell-born schemes, once he had begun the downward slide he could not stop, for autonomy becomes addictive.

There is an irresistible footnote to the Valley of Hinnom. As one stands in the valley and looks upward, the view encompasses what is called the Mount of Offense. It was so called because that is where Solomon housed his harem. There is an inextricable connection between the Mount of Offense and the Valley of Hinnom. The heart fueled by promiscuity will someday fall into the burning arms of an idol that devours our offspring.

Manasseh took a third and final step. There were voices crying out for a halt to what he was doing. One such voice was that of Isaiah the prophet, who paid for his protests with his life. Manasseh instituted a bitter persecution of the prophets, thinking that by silencing them he was doing the politically expedient thing. He did not even bother to look over the historical landscape and learn that he could never succeed in eradicating true spiritual passion by persecuting it. False and superficial beliefs can be stifled by law or power, but those etched into the conscience or soul cannot be obliterated by decree. Somewhere, at some time, they will resurface in public. The words of James Russell Lowell are enduringly true.

> Truth forever on the scaffold,
> Wrong forever on the throne,
> But the scaffold sways the future
> And behind the dim unknown
> Standeth God within the shadows,
> Keeping watch, Keeping watch above His own.[7]

The very prophet that Manasseh killed, Isaiah, was the one who told us more of the Messiah's triumph through suffering and of the everlasting nature of God's kingdom than any other prophetic voice. But for then, with these three deliberate steps, Manasseh changed his country.

This chapter in Judah's experience has some life-affecting lessons to offer to us. First, it proves one of the most repeated lessons in history: *It is possible for one person to lead millions of people into untold evil.* C. S. Lewis pointed out years ago that "man's conquest of nature" was nothing more than the wresting of power by some to control others with the instruments of nature. And for centuries politics has dabbled in the deadly game of social engineering. The whole point of state-controlled education is that it gives to the government the power to shape the souls and write on the fresh slates of young hearts. This empowerment is the most important trust given to elected officers, and to assume that they accept that responsibility from a posture of neutrality is to live under the most destructive illusion. To elect one to the highest level of leadership, therefore, is to put into his or her hands the possibility and opportunity of shaping a nation's conscience.

A few years ago I took part in a discussion with seven military generals at the Center for Geo-political Strategy in Moscow. The imposing structure stands eight stories above ground and descends four stories below ground. As one enters, the ceiling of the welcoming hall towers high above while the massive and highly decorated pictures of all the famous Russian generals throughout history line the walls. Staring into the faces of men like Peter the Great and Mikhail Kutuzov, who led the Russian forces against Napoleon, it is impossible not to feel dwarfed in the historical hall of fame of a superpower nation.

Yet, as we talked about the greatest needs of the hour for the world as a whole, one of the most meaningful moments came, reducing us all to silence, when one of the generals, with an icy stare of hard reality said, "We know what war can do, and we have great fear of it." As we prepared to leave, all seven generals lined up to bid us good-bye.

Then each of them, softened by the hours of interaction, took my wife's hand and kissed it. Finally the chief of staff said to me, "Mr. Zacharias, I believe that what you have said about our need for God is true. But after seventy years of believing a lie it is very hard to change." What a monumental testimony to the power of a handful of individuals seven decades ago who changed the soul of a nation.

I could not help thinking of all that has been done to the Russian people, who are so gifted and capable, by some of their own leaders, and in particular, by Joseph Stalin. During his reign of terror he obliterated fifteen million of his own people. It defies every imagination. Think of his counterpart in Germany, Adolf Hitler, who provoked the bloodiest, most unnecessary, most disruptive war in history and changed the pattern of the world irremediably. Just one person's influence. With that thought, consider the means we now have within our reach by which one person can change history again. If that does not alarm us to the potential consequences when fences have been pulled down, I do not know what will.

THE GULLIBILITY THAT MAKES IT POSSIBLE

The second lesson from Manasseh's life is that *one person is able to lead millions into untold evil only because the nation has ceased to think clearly.* That has been extensively true in the past and is even more pathetically so in the present.

Some years ago ABC news-anchor Ted Koppel delivered the commencement address at Duke University. He daringly challenged the members of the graduating class to hark back to the Ten Commandments and find their moral compass again. In the middle of his talk he made a very pointed reference to America's diminishing capacity to think, glaringly reflected in the heroes our nation creates. (He also, with embarrassment, conceded that his own medium of professional involvement—television—was the principal culprit in producing an unthinking generation.)

In citing Mr. Koppel it is not my intention to cast any aspersion upon the specific person to whom he referred: She herself bears no indictment here, but the unthinking sycophants who swoon at her success strain credulity. To make his point, Koppel coined a new word—"Vannatized"—and then went on to talk about the Vannatization of America, referring to the popularity of game-show assistant Vanna White. Ms. White has done a masterful job, said

Koppel, of turning letters of the alphabet when they light up. She looks utterly enthralled to be doing it, creating such an aura about her in this cerebrally minimal activity that it has brought her a cultic following of national proportions. Her published autobiography sold so quickly it went into a second edition. I repeat, as I echo Koppel's concern, that this befuddling phenomenon says nothing of her. It must not be easy to look so perfectly contented and fulfilled by a feat that does not make much demand on the mind. But how utterly incredible that an activity as minuscule as that should make one a national figure to be adulated—if the pun may be pardoned.

This does say, however, that there are millions out there for whom thinking would indeed be a challenge. And that is why it is possible for one person to lead millions into busy lives with inactive minds. Listen to the horrendous illogic that sounds forth from the gatekeepers of our culture when they try to make a case against the sacred. The argumentative capacity of talk-show hosts who make moral pronouncements against morality is exceeded only by a pathetic inability to build a sound argument. The move from unsubstantiated premises to invalid deductions consistently color their faulty thinking, and what is more, the same fallacies get transmitted to uncritical hearers. Assertions claiming truth frequently go uncorroborated, and the arguments that are built show a complete disregard of validity. One can only shake one's head in disbelief and marvel at how mushy our thinking has become. The science and art of critical thinking have been humiliated in a generation that thinks with its eyes.

THE CRIME THAT FOLLOWED

The greatest lesson Manasseh's life teaches is not just the capacity for one to lead the many nor the incapacity of the many who follow the one. The greatest lesson is that *the ultimate test of any civilization is what we do with our children.*

When the soul of a nation is scarred, its children are part of the loss. Interestingly enough every culture today claims, in theory, to place the highest value on its love of its children. Some time ago when one Middle Eastern leader was asked when the fighting in that part of the world would stop, she answered, "When they love their children more than they hate us." I have little doubt that the opposing side would say the same. There is a profound expression of values in that statement. In our own prisons those whose crime was committed against a child are kept in protective custody to protect them from the anger of other prisoners. Even criminals draw a line. In any course on ethics, the bottom-line illustration is still, "Is it all right to torture babies?" rhetorically stated, of course, and always eliciting a thunderous "Of course not!" In a bizarre way, even in Manasseh's time child sacrifice revealed that the child was of greatest value, and therefore it was offered up to idols of their own making.

Some years ago, I was preaching in a small town in Australia. Sitting close to the front was a woman with two young children. She was somewhat unkempt and bedraggled in her appearance and quite hostile in her expression. Sitting next to her, her little boy fought back tears throughout the entire evening. There was a constant disturbance from their direction with sporadic whispering and threatening gestures from her to the children.

At the end of the service she asked if she could see me alone for a few minutes. She told me she was a convinced Marxist and hated religion with a passion. But because of a promise she had made to a friend, she had come to church that night. Her decision was made on the spur of the moment, and she literally dragged her hastily dressed children into the car. As she sped along through the traffic her son tried to get her attention, but she angrily screamed at him to be quiet. He persisted in trying to get her to just look at him, so she turned around and backhanded him across the mouth, drawing blood, then continued to ignore his sobs and pleas.

Halfway through my message I evidently made a comment about

the hardening or tenderizing role that parents play in their children's lives. Just at that time she caught sight of her son's feet and noticed he was wearing his sister's shoes. She looked at him with bewilderment and asked him why he was not wearing his own. And that is when her private world came apart. She could bottle up her tears no longer as he stuttered out that this was what he had been trying to draw to her attention the whole evening. In her haste, she had grabbed the wrong pair of shoes, and without giving him a chance to tell her they were not his shoes but his sister's, she flung them into the backseat, instructing him to put them on.

The woman herself cried like a child as she talked, acknowledging that her own life was not manageable anymore. Then she muttered, "Dear God, what am I doing to my children?" It became the glorious night that she turned her life over to Christ, and as she walked out into the darkness, she paused to wipe her son's face and left clasping one child in each hand.

The application to our own culture is obvious, is it not? What is it we live for, and what, in that pursuit, are we doing to our own children? One look at the world we are giving to them spells horror. The statistics speak for themselves: In the last fifty years, 149 major wars have been fought, killing twenty-three million people. This figure is double the number of victims of war in the nineteenth century and seven times more than the eighteenth century. The principal victims, of course, are children. In the last decade alone two million children have been killed, four to five million have been disabled, and twelve million have been left homeless. One million have been orphaned or separated from their parents, and ten million have been psychologically traumatized while millions of them have suffered in civil wars such as that in Angola for thirty years, Afghanistan for seventeen years, Sri Lanka for eleven years, and Somalia for seven years.

A whole generation has grown up not knowing a day of peace. In Somalia, for example, more than half of all the children under age five who were alive on January 1, 1992, were dead due to violence by

December 31 of that year. The vortex of violence in which the children are trapped becomes even more horrific when we realize how many of them are now involved in the front lines themselves—literally hundreds of thousands.[8]

Can anyone read these statistics without being overcome? What a price civilization is paying. The statistics in America may be different because we are not engaged in civil war. But we are certainly involved in a moral war that is even more insidious, for it ravages the souls of our children. Greater than the violence in our inner cities is the violation of decency within a child's heart perpetrated by adults. When reason has no point of reference in society the next generation will embody the logic of unreason.

The questions haunt us: What are we doing to our children when we tell them there are no moral boundaries? When we ridicule sacred things? When we leave them vulnerable to any philosophy of life that comes around? When we walk out on marital commitments and leave them defenseless in a predatorial world? What have we done? We have sacrificed them as we have gambled away the sacred and left them to be vandalized by the evil that is present at every stage of life. We have a role in delivering them from evil. But we do havoc to their souls when we tell them there are no fences in life or when we laugh at the proclamation of God's Word. Need one even belabor their victimization in child pornography today? Or recount that scores of children in the inner cities are planning their own funerals at age eight or nine because they do not expect to live to see their teen years? Intellectual capacity can help us to do the surveys and print out the statistics, but only the mind that is disciplined with ultimate values can find answers to these horrible realities. These are questions of the soul.

Some time ago, as I walked into my son's room to kiss him good night, I found him in bed with tears running down the side of his face. I asked him what the matter was. He tried to shrug it off, but at my persistence he finally said, "I am just sorry to be growing out of my childhood so soon. I have enjoyed it so much." What a statement

to be made by a fourteen-year-old on the heels of a wonderful week-
end we had spent together as a family. Contrast these words with the
words of a fourteen-year-old from Bosnia, a young lad named Dinja:

> So many people have been killed fighting for justice. But what justice?
> Do they know what they are fighting for, who they are fighting? The
> weather is growing very cold now. No longer can you hear the singing
> of the birds, only the sound of children crying for a lost mother or father,
> a brother or sister. We are children without a country and without hope.[9]

Children want to be valued, but they also want to know the reason
for that value, and there is no surer way to instill value into them than
to impart to them that they are a gift from God. They are not objects
to be gambled away by spilling them into the destructive arms of the
spirit of the age, arms that have been fashioned by the intellect at
the cost of the mind and soul.

These are the lessons the seventh century B.C. taught Judah. And
in a most incredible turn of events, Manasseh himself fell on his face
before God and repented. But by then a whole generation had been
lost. It was literally the hell of a delayed conversion, for his victims lay
strewn in his path. Personal rescue at the cost of national disaster was
little consolation to him and has a lesson all its own.

By removing the fences he let in a flood of evil ideas. Today with
maverick zeal we debunk the absolute. Can we pause long enough to
think of what we are doing? Hear, for example, the words of noted
scholar Arthur Schlesinger as he touts the brazenness of a society that
is gladly and confidently taking such risks.

In 1989 Schlesinger was asked to speak at the induction of the
president of Brown University. As he presented his challenge, his target was obvious—"the mystic prophets of the absolute":

> The mystic prophets of the absolute cannot save us. Sustained by our
> history and traditions, we must save ourselves, at whatever risk of heresy
> or blasphemy. We can find solace in the memorable representation of
> the human struggle against the absolute in the finest scene in the great-

est of American novels. I refer of course to the scene when Huckleberry
Finn decides that the "plain hand of Providence" requires him to tell
Miss Watson where her runaway slave Jim is to be found. Huck writes
his letter of betrayal to Miss Watson and feels "all washed clean of sin for
the first time I had ever felt so in my life, and I knowed I could pray
now." He sits there for a while thinking "how good it was all this happened so, and how near I come to being lost and going to hell."

Then Huck begins to think about Jim and the rush of the great river
and the talking and the singing and the laughing and friendship. "Then
I happened to look around and see that paper. . . . I took it up, and held
it in my hand. I was a-trembling because I'd got to decide, forever, be-
twixt two things, and I knowed it. I studied a minute, sort of holding my
breath, and then says to myself: 'All right, then, I'll go to hell'—and tore
it up."

That, if I may say so, is what America is all about.[10]

How frighteningly candid. How pathetically wrongheaded. But
before we dismantle all the fences of moral absolutes, we would do
well to listen to the voice from history, the voice of Manasseh. He
speaks to our darkness from the vantage of having made a similar
speech in his time. Thankfully, Manasseh's was not the last chapter in
Judah's history.

Eleven

Restoring the Soul

❦

I LISTENED ON ONE occasion to an informative and impassioned talk on the condition of our large cities around the world. The content ranged from population sizes, criminal activity, social conflicts— all the way down to sewer systems or the lack thereof. As the information quotient was rising something inside me kept crying out, "I agree, I agree, please stop! Just tell us what to do about all of this." The conclusion, when it came in the form of an anecdote, has since provided me with a unit of measurement for an anticlimax.

The speaker related that during the Second World War the British navy was frustrated by the threat of Germany's elusive submarines and was desperate to find a way to spot them before it was too late. A plan was finally offered by one for whom practicality had no value. He suggested that all they would need to do would be to "boil the ocean." He explained, "Once you bring the ocean to a boil, the submarines will be forced to surface. Then we can knock 'em off, one after the other."

"But how does one boil the ocean?" shouted an irritated questioner.

"I don't know," came the reply. "I have just given you the idea; now it is up to you to implement it."

With that quip and a broad smile upon his face, the speaker at our conference sat down. Thankfully, he did not intend to leave the question unaddressed; he was only biding his time to give us an opportunity to reflect on the magnitude of the problem he had presented.

More often than not, cynical solutions are commonplace with so monumental a problem. Such is the problem of wickedness confronting the world. The challenge lies in finding the solution. The Scriptures give us extraordinary insight into this subject of our soul-struggle in a disintegrating culture. Very quickly we notice how God deals with the issue.

Human beings have a limitless capacity to raise the question of the problem of evil as we see it outside of ourselves, but a disproportionate willingness to raise the question of evil within us. I once sat on the top floor of a huge corporate building owned by one of the biggest construction tycoons in this country. Our entire conversation revolved around his question of so much evil in this world and a seemingly silent God. Suddenly interrupting the conversation, a friend of mine said to him, "Since evil seems to trouble you so much, I would be curious to know what you have done about the evil you see within you." There was a red-faced silence.

I have never defended the existence of God at a university campus without being asked about this question of evil in the world. Yet on only one occasion have I been asked how to cope with the evil within. This dichotomy alone gives us a clue as to where it is that God begins to frame the problem and propose a profound answer. As we come to terms with God's response, we will soon detect how it is possible to withstand the most destructive influences of culture and steady the soul in the turbulence of colliding world-views.

The answer will be presented in three phases. First we will see how it has been addressed in the past, so that we may apply it to the present. In the next chapter we will attempt to unravel the mystery of wickedness, and then in the final chapter we will get a glimpse of the power and presence of God even in the darkest manifestations of evil. Such a confrontation seems inevitable as we look at the face of the future.

The man who led Israel to her greatest spiritual recovery, on the heels of Manasseh's evil-ridden reign, was young King Josiah. The Old Testament historian pays him the supreme tribute when he says, "Neither before nor after Josiah was there a king like him who turned to the LORD as he did—with all his heart and with all his soul and with all his strength, in accordance with all the Law of Moses."[1] The four "alls" pretty much tell it all—all his heart, all his soul, all his strength, in response to all the Law of God.

Josiah was only eight years old when he was crowned king. A gentle, but determined little boy, he was to mature into God's ideal of manhood. At age sixteen he passionately sought the mind of God by which to direct his own life. At twenty he realized how Manasseh had turned back the clock Hezekiah had set for the nation's spiritual recovery, and he made his primary goal the restoring of the national soul. His first step was to remove the idols and degrading altars the people had re-erected. Then, at age twenty-six, taking another page from Hezekiah's life, he began the cleansing of the temple, recognizing that its physical disrepair and displaced vision were symptomatic of a lost commitment in the hands of those to whom the people had entrusted their souls.

What a precedent was set by this young leader, eager in his own heart to bring his nation back in tune with the heart and mind of God. His first challenge, therefore, was to those who were in spiritual leadership. That alone tells us what his priority was. Today's leaders are more prone to relish the opportunity to speak before business and financial powerbrokers, making economic concerns of supreme importance. They repeat the seductive blunder of assuming that material comfort will set the nation on a prosperous course. When was the last time a politician up for election called upon the spiritual leadership of the nation to take their calling seriously and lead by example? How heart-stirring it would be for a people and for the youth in particular to see a political leader who cared more for being right than for being elected. Only as those who honor their call before God with responsibility are encouraged and supported will a people turn in similar inclination of spirit with concern for their souls.

By taking these historically proven steps—challenging the false gods of his time and issuing a plea for righteousness to the temple leaders—Josiah stumbled into the most surprising discovery of all. He found the Book of the Law, buried beneath the debris of a neglected temple. How unthinkable this is—that in the midst of the grand edifice whose sole reason for being was the worship of the living God and whose trust was the teaching of the oracles of God, the Word that was central to those purposes was lost under the clutter of ecclesiastical politics. This discovery was providential for Josiah, because there would have been no way for him to usher in a spiritual revival without a keen understanding of the very character of God. For that he needed God's self-disclosure—the Book of Books.

This is the basis on which every nation must structure itself if it is both to understand evil and to deal with it. If a nation does not believe that God has spoken, then all moral points of reference, individually and corporately, become vacuous, and evil will only confound the mind. If, on the other hand, the Scriptures are tested and proven to be what they claim to be, then the soul thrills at the possibility of the grandest freedom of all—deliverance from evil and restoration to unblemished beauty. History has supplied the light upon the stern, and God's Word provides not merely the interpretation of the past but the illumination for our present and the promise for the future.

To this very day when a British sovereign is crowned, as the Bible is placed in his or her hands the words are uttered, "This book is the most valuable thing the world affords." Some years ago, Margaret Thatcher, then British prime minister, did take the example of Josiah when, addressing the Scottish General Assembly of the Church of Scotland, she said to the delegates:

> The truths of the Judaic-Christian tradition are infinitely precious, not only, as I believe, because they are true, but also because they provide the moral impulse which alone can lead to that peace in the true meaning of the word for which we all long. . . . There is little hope for democracy if the hearts of men and women in democratic societies cannot be touched by a call to something greater than themselves. Political structures, state institutions, collective ideals are not enough. We parliamentarians can legislate for the rule of law. You, the Church, can teach the life of faith.[2]

In 1823 Daniel Webster said:

> If truth be not diffused, error will be; if God and His Word are not known and received, the devil and his works will gain the ascendancy; if the evangelical volume does not reach every hamlet, the pages of a corrupt and licentious literature will; if the power of the Gospel is not felt throughout the length and breadth of the land, anarchy and misrule, degradation and misery, corruption and darkness will reign without mitigation or end.[3]

Obviously this presupposes that the Bible is the Word of God. In Appendix A of this book that defense is presented, but we will consider its implication now.

THE GREATEST TREASURE

Few are better equipped to speak on the value of the truth and the place of Scripture than those who have seen the most despotic and tyrannical forms of power or who have been victimized by a culture overtaken by unmitigated evil. Many years ago in Lebanon, I was introduced to a family that was still reeling from the shock of recovered wealth when all seemed hopeless. The way it had come about brought tears and laughter as I heard the story.

Sami, a dear friend of mine, played the hero's role in this touching story. One of Sami's great characteristics was fearlessness. One day he was driving with his wife along a highway on the outskirts of Beirut when he suddenly saw a large suitcase lying on the side of the road. Most people would not only have driven past it, they would have probably picked up speed, almost certain that it was booby-trapped. But not Sami. G. K. Chesterton has defined courage as getting away from death by continually coming within an inch of it. That is a perfect description of Sami.

Much against his wife's pleas, he stopped, walked over to the suitcase, and began to feel its contours.

"Sami," she insisted, "leave it alone and let's go."

She may as well have been talking to a blade of grass. Triumphantly, he shouted back to her, "Joy! I think it is full of something!"

Hardly thrilled by that piece of information Joy called to him once more to come away. But Sami was convinced that somebody had lost it. So, much to his wife's utter anguish, he brought it back to the car and took it home.

To make a fascinating story short, when he opened it, he found every inch of space within crammed with money. It was certainly not the kind of experience that would cause one to moan in despair, "Why me, Lord?" Fortunately, there was also an address and telephone number inside, and after repeated attempts at phoning, someone finally answered. Sami asked for the person by name, and when, in a doleful voice, the man identified himself, Sami asked him, "Sir, have you lost something?"

Taken aback, the man paused and then said, "Have you found it?"

The rest of the story was basically that of a frenzied effort on the part of the man to make arrangements to retrieve his suitcase, which he had lost en route to the boat he was to catch as he was attempting to leave the country.

I was in Sami's home when the owner of the suitcase brought his family to meet, in flesh and blood, a man with a soul in a disintegrating society. Beirut was once called the pearl of the Middle East. Its beauty was both proverbial and historic. Yet in the tangled web of human greed and ideological heartlessness it is a city now where piles of rubble have taken the place of majestic buildings and ancient edifices. In this war-torn suburb a family was dumbfounded to see a life that had not been destroyed by the evil around it.

As they sat in Sami's living room, completely overwhelmed, Sami said gently, "You think you have recovered your treasure. Let me tell you how passing a treasure this is. With the fragile state of our country, this could become completely worthless overnight. Let me give you the greatest and the most enduring treasure you can ever have."

He handed them a copy of the Bible. It was a memorable moment as they held it in their hands. Was this real? Was this the Word of God? Was this indeed the greatest treasure on earth, a light to their feet and a lamp to their path? That was my last glimpse of Beirut, in Sami's home, before I myself set sail for Cyprus the same night, leaving behind a country in physical ruins. But I had witnessed the courage of a man who sought things that are eternal amid the ruins of human wickedness. In his heart he enclosed the city of God in stark contrast to the cities of men.

Indeed, the Bible is not just the trust of monarchs, nor is it just the standard for a nation's conscience. It is the definitive reality of life's purpose, from God's mind to ours. The "Book of the Law" mirrors the soul as it was intended to be. It reveals the sacredness of our words to each other—engendering trust. It holds us to the sanctity of our marital vows—enriching the splendor of love. It preserves the essential dignity of every human being—elevating the beauty of relationships. It bequeaths to us the sacredness of time—enjoining the sanctity of both work and rest. It commands us to respect the property of others—breaking the stranglehold of fear. It guards our essential purpose—energizing us by the coalescence of worship. It is the Mind of God. It is the Law of God. This is not a bondage to rules; this spells deliverance from evil. This was not meant for us to hate;

this was made for us to love. For this we were made: that we might know the mind of God and let that mind dwell in us. This is the Word that calls us to reason together with God so that the evil within us may stir us more than the evil around us. It is only in that sequence that the soul of an individual and the soul of a nation can be recovered.

This is the treasure Josiah gave back to his people—and it is the greatest contribution of the Hebrews to young America as well. Let us be absolutely certain of this. It was not the Code of Hammurabi that touched America's conscience. Nor was it the intent or content of the Koran. By no stretch of imagination was it the pantheistic framework of Eastern mysticism. America's soul was indubitably formed in keeping with the basic assumptions and injunctions of this, the moral law of the Hebrews, which gave her a vision of history's linear thrust whereby she was to reconcile liberty with law.

Let us get beyond the debate as to how orthodox or heterodox the founding fathers were. What is already beyond debate is that the fundamental precepts by which they wanted to govern could only have been possible within a biblical framework, not that of any other major religious system. But in our time the light of the ancient and time-tested blueprint of the soul that Josiah recovered has once again been smothered at the whim of an autonomous culture. The imprints of Athens, Rome, and London are still upon us. But the all-important endowment of Jerusalem has been tossed to the winds.

THE PUREST PURSUIT

Second, Josiah led the people by personal confession and restored to them the beauty and purity of worship. G. K. Chesterton astutely asserted that nothing sublimely artistic has ever arisen out of mere art, any more than anything essentially reasonable has ever arisen out of pure reason. There must always be a rich moral soil for any great aesthetic growth.[4]

Josiah knew that the road back was to put the Law of God into the hands of the people, but maintaining the nation's moral strength required the priority of worship. In this he has once again left an example that political leadership would be wise to follow. Moral convictions rooted in God's nature and in the worship of God are intrinsically related. To be moral for morality's sake becomes a form of self-worship. When the moral law of God is the blueprint for life then the worship that follows shows reverence to the God in whose being that law is revealed. That is the worship that builds strength against evil and triumphs over the fragile will. Nothing involves a greater discipline of the mind than the coherence that worship brings. Who or what a person worships provides the rationale for his or her behavior.

Apart from this moral soil in which people have a reverence for life, the best of minds get channeled in the wrong direction. The concept of moral necessity seems to elude some contemporary intellectuals who brand all moral talk senseless or relative. In reality, all talk outside of a moral context is vacuous. Here we immediately see the first point of variance between the moods of the present and a voice from the past. The debunking of morality by the secularists of our day makes it impossible for either the arts or the sciences to achieve their rightful grandeur. Only in the fertile soil of moral goodness can they truly flourish. And where moral goodness and spiritual hunger are mocked, any harnessing of the strengths of these disciplines is fraught with danger and, indeed, can be cause for fear.

Moral discourse without reverence for life itself is meaningless, and reverence is at the heart of worship. That is why, in one sense, the opposite of *sacred* is not *secular* but *profane*, which literally means "outside the temple." Secularism seeks to establish a cultural base for life apart from the temple, rendering life inside the temple unworthy of serious intellectual respect. The lesson from history is that sanctity within the temple ultimately defines life outside the temple, and without the former, life becomes profane. Just as reverence is at the heart of worship, profanity is at the heart of evil.

This lesson must be driven home because it explains the foundational difference from those who argue for morality without the need for God. Where there is no reverence there cannot be morality, and where there is no God there is no reverence. A world bereft of reverence breeds the very malady now bemoaned by secular intellectuals who seem mystified by what plagues them. Carl Sagan's recent writings are a classic example when he laments the fact that modern day scientists have lost their sense of wonder. Sagan does not seem to grasp the point that they are being more consistent than he is. When the universe is stripped away from a Creator, how long can brute facts enthrall the mind? Ideas have an expiration date for thrills; only the glory of a person is inexhaustible. Wonder can be thrillingly sustained when each new discovery points to the Creator. Without the Creator the means overtakes the end, and wonder dies. Worship is the culmination and continuance of a relationship with a person, not the celebration of an idea.

The same applies to human sexuality. If the sanctity of sexuality is lost, intimacy loses meaning and becomes mere self-gratification. The most demeaning comment ever made on the way sex has been profaned came from an actor who said his relationships have one prerequisite—"If you do not ask me for my name, I will not ask you for yours." The evil contained in such disregard for a person's essential value cannot be denied. Ultimately it is the person behind the relationship that provokes wonder because of the divine image stamped upon the human personality. If the person is a means to an end, then the greater has been destroyed by the lesser. Women who have been betrayed time and time again voice the sense of utter rejection they feel when the means has overtaken the end.

In one of his proverbs Solomon said, "The path of the righteous is like the first gleam of dawn, shining ever brighter till the full light of day" (Prov. 4:18). The only way righteousness can get brighter is when it is based on a relationship and not just on a set of guidelines.

It has been said that society prepares the crime and the criminal commits it. Similarly, genuine worship creates the soil in which society flourishes, and in that soil can be planted a people of peace. Josiah left that soil for his people. When the Law of God was returned to the people and worship was restored, three very direct transformations took place.

One may legitimately argue that this singular vision is possible only in a theocracy, a government that recognizes God as its head—which is what Israel was. That is a correct observation. But we had dare not miss the larger point and the more pertinent lesson of history. What was it that made it possible for a people to turn their backs upon a culture immersed in evil and make a heartfelt change for the good? It was the belief that God had spoken and that life is at its core sacred. Without those two beliefs no society can stem the tide of evil. The place to begin, therefore, is in the individual life. *The soul of a nation is changed one person at a time.* The method may seem slow, but the transformation then occurs with integrity and respect, and the end result is thorough. As we will see, several profound consequences followed from Josiah's two simple steps.

THE CONSOLATION OF THE HEART

First and foremost, the people once again lived with *a sense of safety*. They no longer needed to live in fear of one another or of what might befall them at night in their homes or on their streets. Jewish philosopher Dennis Prager interestingly sustained the connection between reading God's Word and the mitigation of fear when he asked listeners of his radio program the following question: If you were stranded on a lonely road in Los Angeles in the dead of night with your head under the hood of your car, and suddenly you heard the sound of footsteps and turned to see ten burly men walking toward you, would it or would it not make a difference to you if you knew they were coming out of a Bible study? Every caller who responded laughed and granted the deduction.

There are few things our generation longs for more than the confidence to be unafraid of each other. Being a victim is also a state of mind based on the reality that threatens. The billions of dollars we spend on alarm systems, theft-reduction devices, crime-fighting agencies, and weapons with which to defend ourselves tell a pathetic tale of the role fear plays in all of our lives. How glorious it would be to be free from this terrifying reality. That freedom from fear can only come when people love the Law of God and worship Him with reverence. It will not make a perfect world, but it does give our culture a foothold from which to respond to the dangers that lurk.

The evil all around us has cast a net of fear, and we now live perpetually looking over the shoulder. How can life not exact a heavy toll when such stress attends? The conviction of safety is the blessing of a culture at peace with God. Thomas Merton said that man is not at peace with his fellow man because he is not at peace with himself. He is not at peace with himself because he is not at peace with God.

Nearly ten thousand delegates attended the historic Conference for Itinerant Evangelists in Amsterdam hosted by Billy Graham in 1986. At that time, according to a United Nations statistical summary, it was among the largest representation of nations ever gathered. One of the most thrilling stories shared from the pulpit was by a renowned Korean speaker, Billy Kim.

Dr. Kim told of an American soldier hiding in a bunker during a skirmish in the Korean War. When his commander ordered him to scramble closer to the front lines and rescue some of his fallen mates, the soldier nodded his head, took a covert glance at his watch, stalled till his commanding officer was out of sight, and simply made no move. Several minutes went by, and a colleague reminded him of his assignment to rescue those who had fallen. Again he looked at his watch and delayed. Finally, he leaped out of the bunker and fearlessly began the arduous and risky process of carrying his compatriots to safety. At the end of the day when the guns were silent, a friend asked him why he kept looking at his watch when under orders to move. The soldier threw his head back, fighting off the tears, and said, "I was afraid—afraid because I knew I was not ready to die. I lingered for the moment when I knew my fear would be overcome—remembering that at a certain time every hour my mother had said she would pray for me. As soon as that minute struck I knew I was under the shelter of her prayers, and that no matter what awaited me, I could face it."

Who would have imagined that a grown man with so much fire power behind him would find a greater confidence in his mother's prayers? During life's most trying moments there is great comfort in the prayers of one whose life is lived under the shadow of the Almighty. Every time before my wife leaves with me on a trip she agrees on a time with our children when she will be praying for them. That promise has always met with a mutual commitment and obvious gratitude.

When I first heard this story from Billy Kim my mind wandered back to when I was in Vietnam, speaking at a service attended by several American airmen. They were in full uniform, some on alert for missions that were imminent and dangerous. I had already been told that most of them would probably not return. I will never forget that scene as long as I live. The closing hymn resounded throughout the room as these predominantly male voices sang from the depths of the emotions that welled up from within them:

> When Peace like a river attendeth my way,
> When sorrows like sea billows roll,
> Whatever my lot, Thou hast taught me to say:
> It is well! It is well with my soul!

But let us not miss the reason for this peace, stated by the songwriter:

> My sin! Oh the bliss of this glorious thought,
> My sin not in part but the whole:

Is nailed to the cross and I bear it no more
Praise the Lord, Praise the Lord, oh my soul.[5]

Freedom to have peace without begins with the freedom from wickedness within.

General Norman Schwarzkopf of Gulf War fame gathered the largest military arsenal ever assembled in history under his command. Yet, he said that even in the final seconds before the Stealth Bombers began their mission to fire the opening shots of the war and attempt to disable enemy radar, he himself was in prayer with his Bible beside him.

War is a wake-up call to where the real power lies and to what real peace means. In the war of ideas that rages today and amid the restlessness that seems endemic to the national mind-set, we can offer no greater peace than what Josiah gave to his people. The Bible says it with succinct promise: "You will keep in perfect peace him whose mind is steadfast, because he trusts in you" (Isa. 26:3).

THE EMPOWERMENT OF THE WILL

The second benefit of restoring the Law of God was that it gave the people *the power to change*. Our enslavements and indulgences have not only developed into more distasteful appetites; they have also taken from us the power to change. Many confess a craving to change but find themselves helpless and powerless to do so. In refreshing contrast God's Word promises that very power to make the changes we know are right.

Centuries after Josiah, history offers a great illustration of this capacity of God's Word to change lives. One of the most glorious tributes ever paid to the power of the gospel is in the impact it had in the ancient city of Corinth, a little stretch of land that became symbolic of all that was debased and immoral. It is the miracle of the gospel that a church even existed there. Of the twenty-seven books in the New Testament, two of Paul's epistles were addressed to this small city with an international reach.

Historians tell us that Corinth was a city destined for greatness. Strategically located, she took most of the traffic between the north and the south of Greece, and from the east to the west of the Mediterranean. Riches came her way from many directions: balsam from Arabia, carpets from Babylon, slaves from Phrygia, and dates from Phoenicia. However, it was not so much her material wealth that made her a byword among the nations as it was her impoverished spirit. If you had wanted to defame someone as profligate and unfaithful, you would call him or her a "Corinthian." What was it that spoke of her immorality? That story is visible today even in her rubble.

Atop a hill just on Corinth's outskirts sit the remains of the temple of Aphrodite. Aphrodite was thought to be a goddess who, living in continual infidelity to her husband, symbolized promiscuity. Finally he was able to set a trap for her that revealed her wretchedness to all. In Greek mythology we are told that when she was thus exposed, she fled, covering her face in shame. But out of her illicit relationships were born two children, Eros and Phobos, from which we derive the words *eroticism* and *fear*—one an insatiable appetite, the other a paralyzing emotion. How articulate is the past, once again, in its stones and in its lessons.

The temple of Aphrodite housed a thousand prostitutes who descended into the streets of Corinth at night to market themselves to the Corinthian passions. This was Corinth. This was her lewd worship. It is quite an experience to stand there today and remember what the apostle Paul said to the Corinthians when he first arrived. He had just come from Athens, where he had dealt with the questions of the intellect. Here in Corinth, he dealt with the passions of the body. For both, it was the mind that needed renewal. In delineating Corinth's catalog of vices, he graciously added the words, "And as such were some of you." The gospel had changed many a Corinthian, and we can now so clearly understand why it was to them he penned his greatest treatise on the purity of love. Those words stand etched in marble in Corinth to remind the tourist of Paul's text on God's love, which had such transforming power in a context so debauched by erotic love:

> Love is patient, love is kind. It does not envy, it does not boast, it is not proud. It is not rude, it is not self-seeking, it is not easily angered, it keeps no record of wrongs. Love does not delight in evil but rejoices with the truth. It always protects, always trusts, always hopes, always perseveres.
>
> Love never fails. . . .
>
> Now these three remain: faith, hope and love. But the greatest of these is love. (1 Cor. 13:4–7, 13)

How gentle was his touch, how relevant his subject. It was to these very Corinthians, so dead in their sins, that he wrote one of his greatest chapters on the resurrection of Christ. It was to these same Corinthians that he signed off, "with the grace of Christ, the love of God, and the fellowship of the Holy Spirit"—words that spoke of their newfound salvation, their new impetus in worship, and their new bond with each other. That very transforming power of a new love and new desires, God still gives today.

Many years ago when I was speaking in Boston, at the end of a particular message, one of the first persons to respond to the gospel invitation was a young woman. I saw her kneel down and be counseled by one of the pastors on staff. When he had finished, he brought her to meet me and handed me the card she had filled out expressing her desired commitment to Christ. In a complete shock to me, I noticed that under the section marked "profession" she had filled out "prostitute." My expression must have betrayed my surprise, for as I looked at her, she said, "It is true. And I am sorry. In fact, I was on my way to the street I walk every night, feeling so dirty inside but so helpless. I just saw the sign outside this church, saying you were talking on the theme of a new life. I wanted it so badly. God has spoken to me tonight, sir. I leave this place a new woman." In this one life, think of the evil that was stemmed from that night on.

That is the power of God multiplied across centuries in changed lives, lives in which God has brought that difference through His Word. This is the deliverance from evil that begins with the self and not with the philosophical attack upon a disembodied idea of external evil. Is this all just an escapist's haven? Absolutely not. G. K. Chesterton said the problem with Christianity is not that it has been tried and found wanting but that it has been found difficult and left untried. And the change the Word brings is not just a psychological one. The change is that of the mind as it grasps the truth and is not swayed by a mere feeling but by the deliverance deep within.

THE TRIUMPH OF THE MIND

The Word brings not only peace and power but also the third result of Josiah's discovery, which was that it *delivered them from the tyranny of the immediate*. Life can take twists and turns that at times make the best of us despondent as we see the wicked triumph and wonder if there is any purpose to righteousness. We easily become handcuffed by the here and now, or we cry "surrender" to the latest threat voiced by some new ideologue on the cultural landscape. How often we lose heart and hope because of a battle lost to a destructive policy. Despite the importance of these things, our discouragement over bad laws and policies should always be balanced by the larger context of where history has been and where it will inexorably go.

In a shocking turn of events, Josiah was to exemplify the truth that there is more to reality than just one's temporary successes or failures. In something that must have daunted their spiritual march forward, the people saw Josiah's life violently and ruthlessly cut short. They had not envisioned this end to a life so beautifully lived. Where was God in all of this? Where was God? Right in control, teaching them the most difficult of all lessons, that in the ebb and flow of history, pain and disappointment are real. Our moral sensitivity causes us to feel those sharp edges. But the way to victory is in the trust we continue to place in Him who is sovereign over history.

This very principle was embodied in the way Jesus dealt with the wickedness of His time. Author George MacDonald says this of Christ's method of changing society in the face of evil:

> Instead of crushing the power of evil by divine force; instead of compelling justice and destroying the wicked; instead of making peace on earth by the rule of a perfect prince; instead of gathering the children of Jerusalem under His wings—whether they would or would not, and saving them from the horrors that anguished His prophetic soul—He let evil work its will while He lived; He contented Himself with the slow unencouraging ways of help essential; making men good; casting out, not merely controlling Satan. . . . Throughout His life on earth, He resisted every impulse to work more rapidly for a lower good—strong, perhaps, when He saw old age and innocence and righteousness trodden under foot.

MacDonald adds, "To love righteousness is to make it grow, not to avenge it."[6]

Josiah's recovery of the Book of the Law built this kind of righteousness, revived the soul of his people, and gave them God's blueprint for the soul of mankind.

As we witness this drift through history from the Hezekiahs to the Manassehs to the Josiahs of every age, the voices of the past tell us much. Whether it be through the limited philosophy of Greece or in the religious failure of Jerusalem. Whether it be through the tarnished splendor of Rome or the long-set sun of the British Empire, America had better pay heed to these words of Malcolm Muggeridge:

> We look back upon history and what do we see? Empires rising and falling. Revolutions and counter-revolutions. Wealth accumulated

and wealth disbursed. Shakespeare has spoken of the rise and fall of great ones that ebb and flow with the moon. I look back upon my own fellow countrymen, once upon a time dominating a quarter of the world, most of them convinced in the words of what is still a popular song that the God who made them mighty shall make them mightier yet. I've heard a crazed, cracked Austrian announce to the world the establishment of a Reich that would last a thousand years. I've seen a murderous Georgian brigand in the Kremlin, acclaimed by the intellectual elite of the world as wiser than Solomon, more humane than Marcus Aurelius, more enlightened than Ashoka. I have seen America wealthier and more powerful than the rest of the world put together, so that had the American people so desired they could have outdone a Caesar, or an Alexander in the range and scale of their conquests. All in one lifetime. All in one lifetime. All gone. Gone with the wind. England, now part of a tiny island off the coast of Europe, threatened with dismemberment and even bankruptcy. Hitler and Mussolini dead, remembered only in infamy. Stalin, a forbidden name in the regime he helped found and dominated for some three decades. America, haunted by fears of running out of those precious fluids that keep her motorways roaring and the smog settling, with troubled memories of a disastrous campaign in Vietnam and the victory of the Don Quixotes of the media, as they charged the windmills of Watergate. All in one lifetime. All gone.[7]

Muggeridge then brilliantly adds that behind the debris of these solemn supermen and self-styled imperial diplomatists stands the gigantic figure of One because of whom, by whom, in whom, and through whom alone mankind may still find peace: The person of Jesus Christ, He who was the fulfillment of the Law and the object of worship.

Josiah could only show his people the Book. That Book pointed to a Person. The written law could only serve as a mirror and a guide, but Jesus has come to offer us the cleansing of the soul, to define for us the good, to give true freedom by revealing the truth for life's greatest questions, and to grant humanity the strength by which to live. Only by responding to that offer may the soul be steadied and evil understood for what it really is. This now commands our attention.

Part 3

The Face of the Future

Twelve

The Unmasking of Evil

I N 1993 T H E *New York Times Magazine* ran a lead article entitled "The Devil in Long Island." It was a resident's evocative cry, wondering if Long Island was uniquely plagued with some kind of behavioral virus breaking out into an epidemic of horrors unthinkable a generation ago. The assemblage of crimes and victims, of eccentricities and bizarre happenings all under one suburban roof, was truly unnerving: The brutal killings of spouses, the pitiful torture of little Katie Beers, the militant irreverence of Howard Stern, the indulgences of Joey Buttafuoco. Adding intrigue to the long list of those whose lives spun them into the vortex of tabloid delights were Jessica Hahn for her role in the PTL scandal and Walter Hudson. Though not exactly a household name, Hudson needed a casket almost the size of a house for his twelve-hundred-pound body, which was lowered into the ground with the help of a crane. What is it about Long Island, questioned the writer, that endlessly provides grist for the tabloid mill?

The metaphor best suited for Long Island's woes, the author Ron Rosenbaum suggested, was a story that gained international attention—the garbage-laden Islip barge that futilely sought someplace to disgorge its refuse. No one would take it.

> As someone who grew up within the boundaries of Islip Township, watching weeks of coverage of this epic odyssey of humiliation and rejection, I found it hard not to identify with the brave little barge as it was turned away from landfill after landfill all down the Atlantic coast and across the Gulf of Mexico, North Carolina, Florida, Alabama, Mississippi, Louisiana, Texas—all turned it away; then Mexico, Belize and the Bahamas: No one would take Long Island's garbage! It was hard not to feel that what was being enacted was a metaphor, a dramatization of the disdain mainland culture had for Long Island itself.[1]

But here the writer anticipates with sermonic power the self-immunizing mockery of the reader and warns of the contagion:

> Long Island, after all, was supposed to be the future *before* the future. We always had a head start on the life cycle of suburban baby-boom culture because we were the first-born burbs of the baby boom; a burbland created almost all at once, very fast and almost ex-nihilo, right after the war, a self-contained social organism. An organism whose socio-biological clock started ticking a little earlier than subsequent burbs, and whose shrill alarms now seem to signal that it has raced through its mature stage and is now rocketing headlong into the social-organism equivalent of senile dementia.
>
> And so the America that laughs at Long Island's Satanist Demolition Derby, the America that looks down on Long Island as something alien, some exotic, carnivalesque pageant separable from its mainstream because it's separate from the mainland, may have to think again. May have to learn to say of this unruly island what Prospero said of the unruly Caliban at the close of "The Tempest": "This thing of darkness I acknowledge mine."
>
> Because when America laughs at Long Island, it's laughing in the face of its own onrushing future.[2]

Is Rosenbaum right? Is this strip of land with its pockets of perversion only a microcosm of what awaits the rest of the country and possibly the world? It may well be the single issue that calls us all to a common concern.

THE MYSTERY OF EVIL

What will be the face of the future? Futurists dabbling in technology or science delight in the limitless terrain for their speculation. Hardly a week goes by without someone pontificating about the speeds at which we will be flying and the new contraptions we will be using.

Caught up in all these thrilling and, indeed, incredible possibilities, we human beings cavalierly ignore the one element that has plagued us through history but has escalated in this century more than in any other—our chronic bent toward destruction. No incident illustrates this oversight better than the slaughter we have witnessed in Bosnia after the fall of the Berlin Wall. I doubt if there was even one writer anywhere who would have hailed the collapse of the Soviet Union and at the same time envisioned the resultant Bosnian carnage. A catastrophic blind spot that prepared freedom for the people failed to prepare the people for freedom.

The degree of lawlessness and the vulnerability with which we all live was underscored for me in two incidents, minutes apart, on the streets of Moscow. In the first, as we casually walked at midmorning to an engagement, suddenly and without warning, a roving band of gypsies moved to overpower us and ransack our pockets. As we frantically tried to ward them off one member of our group was knocked to the ground. But not one passer-by stopped to help us. While being robbed and possibly injured, to watch yourself becoming a victim, unaided by onlookers, is one of the loneliest feelings in life.

The second incident occurred minutes later, right outside that great symbol of capitalism—McDonald's golden arches—as a crazy, shirtless individual in the biting cold of winter came running along

the sidewalk brandishing a huge butcher knife and threatening anyone in his path. He stopped within inches of me and just stared, eyeball to eyeball. The experience was terrifying but again was made even
worse as an indifferent crowd did not even bother to notice. Life was
too complicated to come to a visitor's aid.

What a drastic change has come upon a nation once so strong in
the eyes of the world. Now there is a powerlessness from within as
social disintegration has left the masses apprehensive of the
newfound freedom for which they had dreamed and hoped for so
long. Little wonder that the gentleman in the military heavily
intoned, "We have no hope to give our young people. They have a
purposeless existence. Can you help us?"

The tragedy is not that of Long Island or Moscow. We are compelled to ask the same questions of the world at large, and how we
answer will ultimately configure the face of the future. First, how do
we respond to what we now call the mystery of wickedness? Every
institution seems powerless to stem the drift into more and more
radically evil behavior. Measured against this grim reality the answer
to this question may well become the acid test of the viability of any
social theory. As the face of evil becomes more hideous and ruthless,
the face of the future becomes more fearsome and dreaded. Yet for
the gospel message this may be the most significant moment in history, for the message of Christ provides the only supernatural hope of
a changed heart and life.

In the plethora of recent books that reveal an unprecedented interest in angels, the average person may miss the fact that some of the
most sophisticated treatments are now being given to this mystery of
evil. Our society is so surrounded by such strange manifestations that
the question of evil can no longer be avoided. In a self-fulfilling prophecy written two years after the article just referred to, Ron Rosenbaum
shifted the locus of violence from Long Island to the nation as a
whole.[3] His treatment of the subject matter may be one of the most
articulate. Yet, by his own admission, in the volume of his analysis he

offers no hope, and what began as a mystery ends as a greater mystery.

For my part, I would like to follow the trail he has opened and try to unveil some of this painful reality. To simplify a complex subject, I would like to present three clues that lead to answers to the mystery of wickedness. As previously stated, this provides the middle ground for the secular and sacred to think together.

IT DOESN'T MAKE SENSE

As one reads Rosenbaum's 1995 article titled "Staring into the Heart of Darkness: Evil Is Back," one is numbed to realize that this is not some distant jungle existence being described. This is Long Island. This is America—her disfigured soul uncovered. The title of the article was prompted by a series of heart-wrenching crimes that victimize those of every age but particularly children and the elderly. This article highlighted not just the catalog of crimes but the brutality and savagery that attended them. What is more, the most pernicious aspect of the discussion was the relational tie of the criminals to their victims.

Who can explain Susan Smith heartlessly drowning her two young children, supposedly to perpetuate an ill-fated love affair? Who can explain the animalistic cannibalism of Jeffrey Dahmer? Who can explain the cold-hearted murder of their parents by Lyle and Erik Menendez? Who can explain the brutal beating and killing of a little two-year-old boy at the hands of a ten-year-old and a twelve-year-old in Liverpool, England? Who can explain the dreadful crimes against at least two teenage girls in St. Catharines, Ontario, when Paul Bernardo tortured, raped, and mutilated them while the sister of one of the victims watched and videotaped it for their later viewing pleasure? Who can explain the honor-roll killings in Fullerton, California, when a handful of Ivy League-bound students bludgeoned one of their classmates to death and then calmly left for a New Year's Eve party? And who can explain the ripping open of a woman's body to wrench the child from her womb and kidnap it? The list seems to be endless and sickening.

How will we give an answer for this? Are we going to stand by and watch our children read of these atrocities and then not talk to them about it until only the most horrendous of crimes will even shock them anymore? I should hope not! It is obvious that answers based on the assumptions of secularism can neither explain nor solve this malady.

In his search for an explanation, Rosenbaum talked to a host of people from scholars and politicians to media personalities. After watching talk-show host Maury Povich interview some contract killers, he contacted Povich, pointing out that "talk shows like Maury's have become the American equivalent of the Athenian agora, where citizens, sophists, and philosophers bat around questions of behavior. They can be barometers of public feeling on questions of good and evil."[4]

Rosenbaum called Mr. Povich to ask him if he had a readout on his audience's perspective on such criminality. Povich had a shocking answer. He said that until recently people excused such criminal acts as child abuse by blaming psychological preconditioners. However, he said, it seemed to him that people were no longer buying these self-exonerating theories as they once had. And he could even pinpoint the moment of change: *When Lyle reloaded.*

What did he mean by that? He was referring to Lyle Menendez, who, having emptied his shotgun into his parents, watched his mother crawl in her own blood as she begged him to spare her life. Instead, he went out of the room, reloaded his gun, and came back to calmly finish her off. That, said Povich, was the turning point for most viewers of his program. They knew this defied reason.

But then his audience was subjected to the next shock. In observing the players behind the violent scenes, viewers began to wonder about the callous and relentless greed that surfaced on the part of those who capitalized on crime. They were completely dumbfounded when they became aware of the money that was being made by opportunists who were marketing Jeffrey Dahmer trading cards and other gimmick-laden products.

Viewers were now visibly angered. Until then they had been willing to concede the possibility that negative factors in a life could contribute to a man or woman going so wrong. But they were outraged by the thought of ordinary human beings heartlessly capitalizing on such bloodthirsty criminal acts. How can it be, they thought, that a civilization could sink so low? They knew with certainty that psychological theory could not explain this dressed-up side of evil. It may be time to tear off the mask and find out what hideousness lies behind the adornment. This may be the face that beckons us to look at the inordinate evil of the human heart.

Here we cautiously pick up our first clue. The question of wickedness widens beyond these few names and popular talk shows. Evil is not just where blood has been spilled. Evil is in the self-absorbed human heart.

IT CANNOT BE ENDURED

This world was dramatically changed after the Second World War. What happened then and what we are doing now only intensifies the question of evil. Perhaps one incident will help us put this into sharper focus. During a recent visit to the Holocaust Museum in Jerusalem, I once again felt the stark horror of the human capacity for evil. But one little activity going on in the back room of the museum drew my attention to the reality behind the exhibits. I watched as young people were riveted, evidently for hours, to the video footage of Adolf Eichmann's trial. Having read detailed accounts of that trial, I, too, stood back for a few moments, watching the expressions on those young faces as the grim details unfolded.

As I watched them I could not help thinking of the outcome of that trial. After all the evidence had been mustered, thousands upon thousands of documents compiled, and Eichmann found guilty, his closing speech summed up the unconscionableness of it all. He had sloganeered his way through the entire trial as the dreadful evidence mounted. Now, moments before his execution, he did the same. This is one journalist's description, as Eichmann walked to his death:

> Adolf Eichmann went to the gallows with great dignity. He had asked for a bottle of red wine and had drunk half of it. He refused the help of the Protestant minister, the Reverend William Hull, who offered to read the Bible with him: he had only two more hours to live, and therefore "No time to waste." He walked the fifty yards from his cell to the execution chamber calm and erect, with his hands bound behind him. When the guards tied his ankles and knees, he asked them to loosen the bonds, so that he could stand straight. "I don't need that," he said when the black hood was offered him. He was in complete command of himself, nay, he was more: he was completely himself. Nothing could have demonstrated this more convincingly than the grotesque silliness of his last words. He began by stating emphatically that he was a Gottgläubiger, to express in common Nazi fashion that he was no Christian and did not believe in life after death. He then proceeded: "After a short while, gentlemen, we shall all meet again. Such is the fate of all men. Long live Germany, long live Argentina, long live Austria. I shall not forget them." In the face of death, he had found the cliché, used in funeral oratory. Under the gallows, his memory played him the last trick; he was "elated" and he forgot that this was his own funeral. It was as though in those last minutes he was summing up the lesson that this long course in human wickedness had taught us—the lesson of the fearsome, *word-and-thought-defying banality of evil.*[5]

Eichmann's last words give us a glimpse into his soul, a soul that was truly wretched. In a very real sense he had not, in fact, forgotten that it was his own funeral; he had just so trivialized evil and made death and destruction so banal that his own funeral was also a frivolous thing. Such is the dire end when the soul makes light of evil. How much more so if a whole culture were to echo that soulless indifference! But that is the danger if we do not define evil in its weighty terms. This has to be the common existential starting ground in a society where secular theory conflicts with the Christian faith. Both despise the violence, and the clues must lead us to a common conclusion.

The mystery of wickedness begins to unravel, does it not? In the first instance we saw the unacceptability of foisting all blame on pre-conditioning psychological factors. Now we see the complete unacceptability of trivializing evil. That is our second joint step. We move to the third.

IT MUST BE DEFINED

A modern-day equivalent to this Eichmann malady is found in a recent movie, *Pulp Fiction*, which I have not seen, nor do I intend to see. But I have heard one scene from it discussed more often than any other. Judging by their comments, most critics, very few excepted, have missed the point. At one place in the story two of the lead characters, Vincent and Jules, are en route to commit a multiple contract murder. As they cruise through Los Angeles, laughing and carefree, they indulge in small talk, discussing what hamburgers and quarter-pounders with cheese are called in France. "Royale with cheese," they chuckle and joke. "Is it because they go by the metric system that they have different names?" asks one of the other. This is the giddy, noth-ing-serious-please theme of their conversation. The average movie-goer leaves the movie with a singular impression—how could they be indulging in small talk when they were about to commit such a dreadful crime?[6]

The point is sorely missed. This is not small talk. This is philo-sophical brainwashing taking place between the two, hitting at the heart of the absolute, insinuating with life-defining implication and application that what we name things is all relative to culture. There is no point of reference. Words are nothing more than culture and convention, conferring different sounds to the same thing. An act or a thing itself has no intrinsic value. *We* decide what to call it. The metric system to one is irrelevant in the imperial system of another. A quarter-pounder with cheese to one is "royale with cheese" to another. "Killing the undefended" to one is "affirming the superior race" to another.

Do we get the point? A shameful act of murder can be trivialized if we rebaptize it "getting even." We can sloganeer our way to the gallows because we may see ourselves as martyrs for autonomous definitions. Bemoaning the banality of evil in Eichmann's disposition, Hannah Arent reminds us that his words were "word-and-thought-defying." Eichmann would have retorted in "*Pulp Fiction* philosophy" that deeds and thoughts are nothing more than word creations.

The farce of that twist on reality is inescapable. Life is not as random as the definition we choose to give it. Words are not puffs of air. We cannot rename wickedness and consider it solved. There is an irrepressible voice, and it is the voice of the soul, which says evil cannot be trivialized. This is what the gospel message is about. This is what the cross is all about. Failing to recognize this has disfigured the soul of America.

Is there a reality that exists outside of mere language, and must our language not then conform to reality? There is a point to the opening verse of John, "In the beginning was the Word." That Word defined reality and the Word of God reminds us time and time again that the heart of man is desperately wicked and that only God is big enough to change it. If we refuse to act on this knowledge, we perfectly fit the description Jesus gave, saying, "If then the light within you is darkness, how great is that darkness!" (Matt. 6:23). On the common ground of acknowledging the mystery of wickedness and on the common conviction that we must know the truth, we find the answer again presented with such force in the Scriptures. Other explanations are no longer convincing.

UNVEILING THE MYSTERY

In summarizing these clues and expressions of evil, we can begin to define what wickedness is. The first component of wickedness is that it is a *fact* of our existence. But wickedness can only be defined in relation to the purpose for which we were created and on the basis of the character of the Creator. Wickedness does not depend on the whims and fancies of a given culture at a given moment. The deviance is always in the context of why God has made us in the first place. If the purpose for life is not known then wickedness can never be defined. This is the reason that all ethical theorizing runs aground if no consensus can be gained on our essence and purpose.

Secondly wickedness has within it the component of *feeling*. Which of us could stand back and read the Susan Smith story and not be aghast at the thought of a mother drowning her own children to pursue a private love affair? In this dimension we come to grips with the agony of evil. The most effective way I can sustain this all-important point is to borrow a very pertinent illustration from C. S. Lewis.

In his book *The Abolition of Man*, the first chapter is entitled "Men Without Chests." No, the title has nothing to do with an Arnold Schwarzenegger build or the lack thereof but with a profound warning of where society is headed if our educational theories fail in teaching children about right and wrong. Lewis tells of a book he had read. Not being one to attack another person or even to respond to any criticism when he was criticized, Lewis called the book "The Green Book" and referred to its authors as Gaius and Titius. The book is about teaching children how to think about morality.

In their second chapter, Gaius and Titius quote the well-known story of Coleridge at the waterfall, describing the response of two tourists to that spectacular sight. Coleridge reported that one called it sublime, and the other called it pretty—and Coleridge echoed the first tourist's judgment as the right one. But here Gaius and Titius go to great lengths to challenge Coleridge by saying that a waterfall is not sublime; the tourist was merely describing his *feelings*, which were sublime, because sublimity, they contend, does not exist as a reality outside of feeling.

Lewis is stirred by this bizarre notion of Gaius and Titius and mounts a tremendous counterpoint. He says there is no way feelings could be thus dismissed as glandular or just plain reaction that says nothing about reality. If anything, the sight of a gigantic waterfall renders a sense of smallness and humbleness in the viewer at seeing something so massive, beautiful, powerful, and spectacular. One's feelings are no more merely sublime feelings than calling one contemptible would mean that I have contemptible feelings.

Lewis goes to great length to explain that goodness and badness have corresponding realities and are not merely physiological conditions. Some things thrill because they ought to. Some things hurt because they must. Some relationships ought to inspire and do. Witnessing a brutal murder must cause us to shudder. Watching a beautiful child chuckling in its mother's arms is delightful.

But alas! What have we done to ourselves? We have told a generation that science is real and therefore the human brain is real. We have told them that food is real and therefore our stomachs are real. But we have told them that good and bad do not exist and therefore our emotions have nothing to do with reality. In effect we have produced a generation of "men with brains and men with stomachs. Men with no heart. Men without chests." Now as we witness wickedness at its worst we wonder how the criminal could be so heartless. "In a sort of ghastly simplicity we remove the organ and demand the function. We make men without chests and expect of them virtue and enterprise. We laugh at honor and are shocked to find traitors in our midst. We castrate and bid the geldings be fruitful."[7]

The failure of the perpetrator of wickedness to feel emotion is the result of a society that has trained itself not to feel guilty when wrong is committed.[8]

In biblical terms, encountering wickedness must of necessity engender a feeling of brokenness for both the perpetrator and the victim of the deed. That is why after his sin David compared his inner state to that of a man with broken bones aching within him. "When I kept silent, my bones wasted away through my groaning all day long. For day and night your hand was heavy upon me; my strength was sapped as in the heat of summer. Then I acknowledged my sin to you . . . and you forgave the guilt of my sin" (Ps. 32:3–5). In keeping with the comfort of forgiveness, that psalm begins with "Blessed [happy] is the man whose sin [is forgiven]." One can see in this soul-wrenching prayer why David is called a man after God's own heart. God has given us emotions that conform to reality. Let us be sure that emotion is not in itself a judgment upon reality. In that sense the emotions are alogical. But certainly they must conform to reason and obey it.

At a recent meeting I was addressing in Hong Kong, a businessman stood up and proposed that all values were just contrived and had no bearing on ultimate reality. After I answered his question, I invited him to come and have a personal talk on the subject. He took me up on the offer, and with a crowd of people straining their necks to listen in on the conversation, I said to him that by inference one could assume that he denied that any act was intrinsically evil.

"That is a correct inference," he said.

Hardly believing the hole he had dug for himself, I asked him the obvious. "Suppose I were to take a newborn baby, bring it to this platform, and proceed with a sharp sword to mutilate that child. Are you saying to me that there is nothing actually wrong or evil in that deed?"

To the stunned expressions of those listening in he shrugged and shifted and then said, "I may not like it, but I cannot call it morally wrong."

There was only one thing left to say. "How incongruous it is, even by your own philosophy, that while denying the fact of evil you are unable to completely shake off the feeling . . . for even you, sir, said you would not like it. An understatement I hope." The conversation suddenly took a dramatic turn on how one can know ultimate reality, because he had mangled his own.

This brings us to the third component of wickedness, and that is the *face* of evil. God never describes wickedness as a vaporous idea or appends it to a nameless, faceless throng. Evil is always personal, and the one who acts wickedly is responsible. In these three components of wickedness—the fact, the feeling, and the face—we can readily see why secular society calls it a mystery. With a philosophy of life that has removed objective moral standards and lost any purpose for existence, there is no fact. With a philosophy of life that has severed emotion from value, there is no feeling. With a philosophy of life that does not want anyone to take responsibility for anything but passes the blame onto someone or something else, there is no face. Wickedness that is fact-less, feeling-less, and face-less will ever remain a mystery.

God's Word makes no such blunder. The mystery is removed when we see wickedness as God sees it and when we see ourselves as God sees us. Evil is real. Feelings must conform to what is real. Personal responsibility is indispensable in dealing with the perpetrators of evil.

THE GROUNDING OF REALITY

Now contrast the bewildering unfeeling and unthinking bravado of Eichmann, going to the gallows trivializing evil, with the thoughts of Dietrich Bonhoeffer, going to his death because he took a daring stand against Hitler. Listen to the words of Bonhoeffer on the nature of good and evil and on the only source for right definitions. He penned these words after he, too, had witnessed the most blatant forms of wickedness renamed under the banner of nationalism:

> The great masquerade of evil has played havoc with all our ethical concepts. For evil to appear disguised as light, charity, historical necessity, or social justice is quite bewildering to anyone brought up on our

traditional ethical concepts, while for the Christian who bases his life on the Bible it merely confirms the fundamental wickedness of evil.

The "*reasonable*" people's failure is obvious. With the best intentions and a naive lack of realism, they think that with a little reason they can bend back into position the framework that has got out of joint. In their lack of vision they want to do justice to all sides, and so the conflicting forces wear them down with nothing achieved. Disappointed by the world's unreasonableness, they see themselves condemned to ineffectiveness; they step aside in resignation or collapse before the stronger party.

Still more pathetic is the total collapse of moral *fanaticism*. The fanatic thinks that his single-minded principles qualify him to do battle with the powers of evil; but like a bull he rushes at the red cloak instead of the person who is holding it; he exhausts himself and is beaten. He gets entangled in non-essentials and falls into the trap set by cleverer people.

Then there is the man with a *conscience*, who fights single-handed against heavy odds in situations that call for a decision. But the scale of the conflicts in which he has to choose—with no advice or support except from his own conscience—tears him to pieces. Evil approaches him in so many respectable and seductive disguises that his conscience becomes nervous and vacillating, till at last he contents himself with a salved instead of a clear conscience, so that he lies to his own conscience in order to avoid despair; for a man whose only support is his conscience can never realize that a bad conscience may be stronger and more wholesome than a deluded one.

From the perplexingly large number of possible decisions, the way of *duty* seems to be the sure way out. Here, what is commanded is accepted as what is most certain, and the responsibility for it rests on the commander, not on the person commanded. But no one who confines himself to the limits of duty ever goes so far as to venture, on his sole responsibility, to act in the only way that makes it possible to score a direct hit on evil and defeat it. The man of duty will in the end have to do his duty by the devil too.

As to the man who asserts his complete *freedom* to stand foursquare to the world, who values the necessary deed more highly than an unspoilt conscience or reputation, who is ready to sacrifice a barren principle for a fruitful compromise, or the barren wisdom of a middle course for a fruitful radicalism—let him beware lest his freedom should bring him down. He will assent to what is bad so as to ward off something worse, and in doing so he will no longer be able to realize that the worse, which he wants to avoid, might be better. Here we have the raw material of tragedy.

Here and there people flee from public altercation into the sanctuary of *private* virtuousness. But anyone who does this must shut his mouth and his eyes to the injustice around him. Only at the cost of self-deception can he keep himself pure from the contamination arising from responsible action. In spite of all that he does, what he leaves undone will rob him of his peace of mind. He will either go to pieces because of this disquiet, or become the most hypocritical of Pharisees.

Who stands fast? Only the man whose final standard is not his reason, his principles, his conscience, his freedom, or his virtue, but who is ready to sacrifice all this when he is called to obedient and responsible action in faith and exclusive allegiance to God—the responsible man, who tries to make his whole life an answer to the question and call of God. Where are these responsible people?[9]

This is a clarion call to the West, which has seen so much bloodshed. We can only stand our ground, not on the shifting theories of human ingenuity, but on the blueprint of the Creator. When we see our hearts as God sees them, we find His strength, not only to understand good and evil, but to act on it. The one who resists this truth has nowhere to turn.

Thirteen

The God Who Is Near

THE GRANDEUR of the gospel strikes deep into the soul of wickedness because it offers not merely an analysis of the condition nor just the strength to do what is right; it goes to our innermost being, where the work of God changes what we want to do. This is not an ethical system calling us to civility. This is the transforming work of the grace of God, who then deigns to call us His children.

Charles Wesley said it well:

> Long my imprisoned spirit lay
> Fastbound in sin and nature's night;
> Thine eye diffused the quickening ray.
> I woke, the dungeon flamed with light;
> My chains fell off, my heart was free;
> I rose, went forth, and followed thee.[1]

This transformation can only take place when evil is fully faced for what it truly is and the soul is bought back from under its control.

Only One was capable and willing to pay the price—the Lord Jesus
Christ.

HIS TRANSFORMING POWER

Joseph Damien was a missionary in the nineteenth century who min-
istered to people with leprosy on the island of Molokai, Hawaii.
Those suffering grew to love him and revered the sacrificial life he
lived out before them. But even he did not know the price he would
pay. One morning before he was to lead them in their daily worship,
he was pouring some hot water into a cup when the water swirled out
and fell onto his bare foot. It took him a moment to realize that he
had not felt any sensation. Gripped by the sudden fear of what this
could mean, he poured more boiling water on the same spot. No feeling whatsoever.

Damien immediately knew what had happened. As he walked
tearfully to deliver his sermon, no one at first noticed the difference in
his opening line. He normally began every sermon with, "My fellow
believers." But this morning he began with, "My fellow lepers."

In a greater measure Jesus came into this world knowing what it
would cost Him. He bore in His pure being the marks of evil, that
we might be made pure. "For this I came into the world," He said
(John 18:37).

R. S. Thomas poignantly captured the significance of Jesus' sacrifice to accomplish our redemption in his poem, "The Coming."

And God held in His hand
A small globe. Look, He said.
The son looked. Far off,
As through water, He saw
A scorched land of fierce
Colour. The light burned

There; crusted buildings
Cast their shadows; a bright
Serpent, a river
Uncoiled itself, radiant
With slime.

       On a bare
Hill, a bare tree saddened
The sky. Many people
Held out their thin arms
To it, as though waiting
For a vanished April
To return to its crossed
Boughs. The son watched
Them. Let me go there, he said.[2]

The gospel points to the person of Christ who went to the cross, not just to transform the Jeffrey Dahmers and the money-grabbers behind the scenes, but to renew even those whose self-righteousness blinds them to their own need. It was not just the prodigal in the far-off country who squandered the love of the father; the older brother lost out as well, though he was so close to the father's love. The treasure is within reach of America—the treasure of her recovered soul.

HIS PERSONAL INVITATION

How a culture responds to the cross will determine its face for the future, for the cross alone can transform the heart. But a second question arises: How is it possible to live in a world that will ever swing between extremes, possibly finding newer and more expeditious ways of multiplying evil? Just as the Word of God is definitive in explaining the human heart, that same Word must connect our lives through turbulent times—times past and times to come.

The Word was the instrument Jesus used to counter evil in His own wilderness experience. As Satan taunted Jesus and tried to persuade Him to compromise the greatest good for a seemingly innocent moment of self-glorifying power, Jesus responded to every distortion of the good with the simple words: "Be gone. It is written." This confidence in God's Word not only instructs us in our battles against wickedness but puts into perspective the short-lived emotional impact of even the greatest victories. Only the written Word transcends every experience, good and bad.

The writers of the Scriptures are very clear on this. I turn to one of the greatest experiences ever vouchsafed to the human eye, the transfiguration of Jesus. The three disciples who were with Him saw His countenance glow as His face shone like the sun and His clothes became as white as light. They saw Moses and Elijah descend from the heavens and talk to Jesus. They heard a voice from heaven as the voice of God Himself testified, "This is My Son; listen to Him." The three disciples fell on their faces, and when they had gathered their composure, Peter predictably beseeched Jesus that they ought to stay there forever and not go down to the city again. But Jesus unhesitatingly reminded him that there was work to be done and that the glorious experience was no substitute for the reality that surrounded them till the eternal reality would come.

We must bear in mind this mountaintop experience of Peter's if we are to understand the depth of the truth he stated when he himself referred back to this high point in his life. He says this in his letter to fellow Christians.

We did not follow cleverly invented stories when we told you about the power and coming of our Lord Jesus Christ, but we were eyewitnesses of his majesty. For he received honor and glory from God the Father when the voice came to him from the Majestic Glory, saying, "This is my Son, whom I love; with him I am well pleased." We ourselves heard this voice that came from heaven when we were with him on the sacred mountain.

[But] we have the word of the prophets made more certain, and you will do well to pay attention to it, as to a light shining in a dark place, until the day dawns and the morning star rises in your hearts. Above all, you must understand that no prophecy of Scripture came about by the prophet's own interpretation. For prophecy never had its origin in the will of man, but men spoke from God as they were carried along by the Holy Spirit. (2 Pet. 1:16–21)

This is a most remarkable passage. What Peter is saying here in the context of the exhilaration of being present at the transfiguration is that every experience, however enthralling, must ultimately be seen as temporary. Only the Word of God exceeds the message of the moment and transcends all time. Christians live dangerously when experience is the final authority. The skeptics knew what they were doing when they attacked the Bible because they knew experience alone could easily be explained away, sometimes even by the one who lived the experience. If the critic can reduce all of Christianity to a "religious experience" unverifiable by any other means, then we are confined to a privatized belief with no objective authority left to defend. By being preoccupied with mountaintop experiences or being overcome by the face of evil, the Christian robs himself or herself of the greater treasure of the Word of God "made more certain."

Does this negate the value of experience? Absolutely not. It merely puts into perspective how every experience must point beyond itself to that by which it can be measured. This transtemporal certitude of the Word will carry us through the roller-coaster journey of human fickleness and experiential limitation. Our confidence is in His sovereignty over our nations and over history. But even beyond that we know that His care is personal even in the most turbulent times.

This Word reminds us that there is only one Eternal City. As the barbarians scaled the walls of his beloved city, Augustine wept and penned *The City of God*. No, Rome was not the eternal city. As Athens sowed the seeds of its own destruction, Socrates chose to drink the hemlock rather than give up his pursuit of the virtuous. In

England Wordsworth wept for the return of Milton to address the loss of England's heroic character. Jesus wept at the sight of His beloved city and said, "If you . . . had only known on this day what would bring you peace—but now it is hidden from your eyes" (Luke 19:42).

Rome, Athens, and Jerusalem have all lost their ancient glory. Today our alabaster cities have become tarnished, and with eyes dimmed by tears we cry, "Deliver us from evil." But that deliverance can come only if we respond to the Creator's loving invitation:

> Come to me, all you who are weary and burdened, and I will give you rest. Take my yoke upon you and learn from me, for I am gentle and humble in heart, and you will find rest for your souls. (Matt. 11:28–29)

> Come, all you who are thirsty,
>   come to the waters;
> and you who have no money,
>   come, buy and eat! . . .
> Why spend money on what is not bread,
>   and your labor on what does not satisfy?
> Listen, listen to me and eat what is good,
>   and your soul will delight in the richest of fare.
> Give ear and come to me;
>   hear me, that your soul may live. (Isa. 55:1–3)

If we can say, with King David, "As the deer pants for streams of water, so my soul pants for you, O God," our deliverance is at hand.

HIS IMMEASURABLE GRACE

As I bring this book to a close, let us look back over the long journey we have come through. In contrast to the secularizing influences that have disoriented our culture, we return to the precious truth of God's revelation. Throughout history the Word of God has remained firm; it rises up to outlive its pallbearers. The following story probably stirs my own confidence in God's sovereignty and the power of His Word through troubled times more than any other I know. The circumstances and the particulars are overwhelming.

During my ministry in Vietnam in 1971, one of my interpreters who traveled with me was Hien Pham, an energetic, devoted young Christian who had worked very closely as a translator with the American military forces, purely as a civilian, with no official or military responsibilities. He just knew English so well that he was able to be of immense help to them in their linguistic struggles.

By virtue of that same strength he also worked with the missionaries. He and I traveled the length of the country and became very close friends before I bade him good-bye when I left Vietnam to return home. We were both very young, and neither of us knew if our paths would cross again. Within four years Vietnam fell, and Hien's fate was unknown.

Seventeen years later, in 1988, I received a surprise telephone call that began with, "Brother Ravi?" Immediately I recognized Hien's voice. We got caught up with our pleasantries, then I asked him how he had managed to get out of Vietnam and come to the United States. I was not prepared for the story I was about to hear.

Shortly after Vietnam fell to the Communists, Hien was arrested. Accused of aiding and abetting the Americans he was in and out of prison for several years. During one long jail term, the sole purpose of his jailers was to indoctrinate him against the West—and especially against democratic ideals and the Christian faith. He was cut off from reading anything in English and restricted to communist propaganda in French or Vietnamese. This daily overdose of the writings of Marx and Engels began to take its toll on him. One of the books he was given to read pictured the communist man as a bird in the ironclad cage of capitalism, throwing itself against the bars of "capitalist oppression" and bloodying itself in the process. Yet still it continued to struggle in its quest for freedom.

Hien began to buckle under the onslaught. *Maybe*, he thought, I *have* been lied to. Maybe God does *not* exist. Maybe my whole life *has* been governed by lies. Maybe the West *has* deceived me. The more he thought, the more he moved toward a decision. Finally, he made up his mind. He determined that when he awakened the next day, he would not pray anymore or ever think of his Christian faith again.

The next morning, he was assigned to clean the latrines of the prison. It was the most dreaded chore, shunned by everyone, and so with much distress he began the awful task. As he cleaned out a tin can filled to overflowing with toilet paper, his eye caught what he thought was English printed on one piece of paper. He hurriedly washed it off and slipped it into his hip pocket, planning to read it at night. Not having seen anything in English for such a long time, he anxiously waited for a free moment. Under his mosquito net that night after his roommates had fallen asleep, he pulled out a small flashlight and shining it on the damp piece of paper he read at the top corner, "Romans, Chapter 8." Literally trembling with shock, he began to read:

> And we know that in all things God works for the good of those who love him, who have been called according to his purpose. . . .
> What, then, shall we say in response to this? If God is for us, who can be against us? He who did not spare his own Son, but gave him up for us all—how will he not also, along with him, graciously give us all things? . . .
> . . . Who shall separate us from the love of Christ? Shall trouble or hardship or persecution or famine or nakedness or danger or sword? . . . No, in all these things we are more than conquerors through him who loved us. For I am convinced that neither death nor life, neither angels nor demons, neither the present nor the future, nor any powers, neither height nor depth, nor anything else in all creation, will be able to separate us from the love of God that is in Christ Jesus our Lord. (Rom. 8:28, 31, 32, 35, 37–39)

Hien wept. He knew his Bible, and he had not seen one for so long. Not only that, he knew there was not a more relevant passage of conviction and strength for one on the verge of surrendering to the threat of evil. He cried out to God, asking for forgiveness, for this was to have been the first day in years that he had determined not to pray. Evidently the Lord had other plans.

The next day, Hien asked the camp commander if he could clean the latrine again. He continued with this chore on a regular basis, because he had discovered that some official in the camp was using a Bible as toilet paper. Each day Hien picked up a portion of Scripture, cleaned it off, and added it to his nightly devotional reading. In this way he retrieved a significant portion of the Bible.

The day came when, through an equally providential set of circumstances, Hien was released. He promptly began to make plans to escape from the country. After several unsuccessful attempts he began again to build a boat in secret. About fifty-three other people planned to escape with him, and Hien was taking the lead. All was going according to plan until a short while before the date of their departure when four Vietcong knocked on Hien's door. When he opened it, they accosted him and said they had heard he was trying to escape. "Is it true?" they demanded. Hien immediately denied it and went on to distract them with some concocted story to explain his activities. Apparently convinced, they reluctantly left.

Hien was relieved but very disappointed with himself. "Here I go again, Lord, trying to manipulate my own destiny, too unteachable in my spirit to really believe that You can lead me past any obstacle." He made a promise to God, fervently hoping that the Lord would not take him up on it. He prayed that if the Vietcong were to come back again, he would tell them the truth. Resting in the comfort of that impossibility, he was thoroughly shaken when only a few hours before they were to set sail the four men stood at his door once more. "We have our sources, and we know you are trying to escape. Is it true?" Hien resignedly gave his answer, "Yes, I am, with fifty-three others. Are you going to imprison me again?" There was a pronounced pause. And then they leaned forward and whispered, "No. We want to escape with you!"

In an utterly incredible escape plan, all fifty-eight of them found themselves on the high seas, suddenly engulfed by a violent storm. Hien fell with his face in his hands, crying out to God, "Did You bring us here to die?"

As he concluded his story, he said, "Brother Ravi, if it were not for the sailing ability of those four Vietcong, we would not have made it." They arrived safely in Thailand, and years later Hien arrived on American soil where today he is a businessman—forever grateful for America and praying that she would open her heart as a nation to Christ.

The famed poet William Cowper wrote:

> God moves in a mysterious way
> His wonders to perform;
> He plants His footsteps in the sea,
> And rides upon the storm.
>
> His purposes will ripen fast,
> Unfolding every hour:
> The bud may have a bitter taste,
> But sweet will be the flower.
>
> Blind unbelief is sure to err,
> And scan His works in vain:
> God is His own interpreter,
> And He will make it plain.[3]

How marvelous is the grace of God who has proven again and again that His Word brings light to a dark place, and who can take the wrath of men to bring praise to His name. The artist who spoke to Dorian Gray was right. The Bible does say, "Come now, let us reason together. Though your sins are like scarlet, they shall be as white as snow; though they are red as crimson, they shall be like wool" (Isa. 1:18). Killing the artist is but to kill the voice of reason.

WHAT A MOMENT; WHAT A POSSIBILITY

That is the invitation to the great country of America and to every nation and culture of the world. Churchill once said something to the effect that Americans would always do the right thing . . . after trying everything else first. There are some glorious signs on the horizon. Businessmen and women are responding in large numbers today to the gospel. There are home Bible studies in the tens of thousands. Young people in schools and universities are openly talking about spiritual matters. Many churches in Canada, the United Kingdom, and America are beginning to sense renewal. Our prayer can be concerted and confident. One can only imagine the impact the world over when the threatened soul of Western culture finds the light of Christ and is transformed by His life.

The words uttered by the frightened American cringing under God's judgment in Hermann Hagedorn's *The Bomb That Fell Over America* are most appropriate:

Me, Lord? . . . How odd! I'm sure you must be mistaken.
There's nothing the matter with *me*.
It's the other fellow that's the trouble, a hundred and thirty-
     five million of him.

          . . . . .

The Lord said not a word . . .
I felt a Hand on my collar, a hand that made me remember
The woodshed and the shingle, and the glint in a father's eye.

          . . . . .

The Lord bent down over me as a mother bends over a baby.
"You are a child," said the Lord, "and
My heart is sick with your childness.
But you have a soul, and I've found you just never can tell.
If I could get by your ego, and somehow crack open your
     nucleus—
Something might happen . . . And there is a world at stake.[4]

The Ineradicable Word

AT THE 1995 Mayoral Prayer Breakfast in Washington, D.C., ten-year-old Ashley Danielle Oubré, delivered a memorable speech that brought the audience to its feet in two standing ovations. The brief but mind-stirring text follows.

Good morning, Mayor Barry, platform guests, ladies, and gentlemen. I appreciate this opportunity to speak to the leadership of the greatest city in the world on behalf of the children. I wondered what I would say to you when I was first asked if I would make a presentation. Being young limits the experience you have in most areas, but not as being a child.

Jesus said, "Unless you become like a child you cannot enter the kingdom." When I think about my friends, who are all young people like myself, many things come to mind.

If you would like to be a child in God's kingdom, I will share some of what we think about and do.

Children play together, have lots of fun, and sometimes fight, but the very next day we make up and play again. Wouldn't it be wonderful if mothers and fathers, sisters and brothers, neighbors and our leaders would be more that way? It hurts us when we see you fighting and not making up.

When you tell us something, we believe it, and we don't ask many questions. We have faith and trust in you until we grow up and find it's really not that way with adults. I think you tell us Bible stories because we are children. The Bible stories do us a lot of good, but you don't tell each other Bible stories. Are they only good for children?

You teach us that when we have a problem, we should talk it out with others and with Jesus. You say that we should pray about it and keep our hearts right for Jesus. You say that Jesus can solve all of our problems, both big and small. But we notice, when people get older and have problems, they are embarrassed to talk like that among themselves. We wonder if you really mean it, or is Jesus only for kids? I am still young enough to believe that Jesus knows how to solve my problems, the problems of the city, and of the world. I hope I never grow old enough to stop believing and that you all become like children in search of God's kingdom.

Thank you very much for listening to me. God bless you all![1]

The easiest response by a skeptic, even to such innocence, would be to dismiss this as childish simplicity at best, wandering in uncharted terrain and eliciting sentimental applause. But let us be clear of the adult-sized ramifications of this child's questions. Is the Bible merely a fanciful storybook, distorting reality? Or is it fantastically true, challenging the intellect against its escapist illusions? Is there truth for all of us within its pages, or is it only for those with superstitious and unsuspecting minds? Is this indeed the Word from God to us, or is it the fraudulent work of a few claiming divine superintendency?[2]

There is absolutely no doubt that the Christian message stands or falls upon the authenticity or spuriousness of the Bible. Believing it to be God's Word, millions across history have staked their lives upon it; destiny-defining trust has been placed in it; graveside hope has been based upon it; extraordinary good has been spread because of it; the charters of nations have been built upon it; others with equal intensity have sought to expel it; yet wrongheaded zeal has caused untold evil in its name. There is no book in history that has been so studied, so used, and so abused as the Holy Bible. How life-inspiring it would be to many more if only they could be indubitably certain of its truth. Can we muster the courage to face up to its claims of divine authorship?

Many routes could be taken in the defense of the uniqueness and authority of the Bible. The age-old approach would be to test its accuracy by measuring the authenticity of the present text of the Scriptures against the earliest extant documents. In such a venture scholars examine the text of Scripture as they would examine any document, investigating such things as authorship, date, historical reliability, and acceptability at the time of writing. This approach is obviously foundational because if these matters cannot be verified all else must stand on a leap of faith.

In addition, the supernatural nature of the content is important to consider, for example, miraculous claims such as fulfilled prophecies and the ultimate assertion of Christ's divinity and power in His resurrection from the dead. Still other buttressing factors—such as the sheer volume of early manuscripts, which is unmatched by any other writing of such antiquity—make the evidentiary basis quite overwhelming. When the archaeological and philosophical defenses are added to these arguments, a very powerful case can and has been made for trusting the Bible to be what it claims to be.

Instead of dealing with the question in the traditional way, because much is already available in that genre, my present response focuses on the authority of the Bible in the existential struggles of life, particularly as we cope with evil.

THE PERFECT ENDORSEMENT

First and foremost, the Bible is the only book in the world that points to a life perfectly lived amidst the grim realities and alluring forces of human existence. Pore over the countless pages written across time, and it becomes quickly evident that the founders of various religions or cults fall short in their own lives, not only when measured against the supreme standard of the Law of God, but even when measured by the standards they themselves have espoused. Biographical sketches of some who today have a following in the millions should only make one wonder how lives so poorly and immorally lived could be so revered.

In contrast to all of them, the life of Christ stands supreme and impeccable. The recognition of this uniqueness in the person of Christ has been readily expressed by some of history's greatest scholars, both those who are avowedly Christian and those distinctly non-Christian. (An example of the latter would be the historian W. E. H. Lecky who, in *A History of European Morals from Augustus to Charlemagne II*, granted the impact of Christ as unequaled in word and deed.)

So incredible is this unblemished life that, in an effort to make his own defeated aspirations seem normal, the noted intellectual Nikos Kazantzakis, in his novel *The Last Temptation of Christ*, tried desperately to construct a Christ who succumbed to the impulse of sensuality. Kazantzakis failed in his pathetic bid because he robbed himself of the life-changing truth that it was Christ's purity that made His empowering grace possible, not the indulgence Kazantzakis tried to fabricate.

How grand is a life so perfectly lived, a life that resisted every enticement of lust, greed, and power even in its most seductive forms. Pontius Pilate, the power seeker, said of Him, "I find no fault in this man." The convicted criminal hanging by Him said of Jesus, "This man has done nothing amiss." The religious leaders who saw Him as a threat to their demagoguery mounted the farcical charge that He was healing on the Sabbath and therefore He was ceremonially vile.

Is it any wonder that even the outcasts of society clamored for His spotless presence and that a devout though rich man like Joseph of Arimathea offered a tomb for His burial? A learned man like

Nicodemus sought Him out because he saw in Him a wisdom beyond anyone he had ever known. He whose dwelling was in the heavenlies attracted even those whose lives were marred and scarred by every pollution of the earth.

This One who lived with such perfection pointed to the authority of the Word when He said, "The Scripture cannot be broken." He spoke of the eternality of the Word when He said, "Heaven and earth shall pass away, but my words will never pass away." He pointed to the centrality of the Word when the Devil tried to tempt Him in the subtlest form of evil—to use His power for self-aggrandizement rather than for the honor of God. The Word reflected the character of God. That reflection was merely propositional in the Scriptures, but it was lived out in the life of Jesus. What good would the Law have been if its very author could not demonstrate its purity?

At the 1994 Presidential Prayer Breakfast in Washington, D.C., Mother Teresa delivered a soul-searching address in which she touched upon the sensitive theme of abortion. When a reporter afterword asked President Clinton what he thought of her remarks he simply stated, "It is very hard to argue against a life so well lived." If the life of Mother Teresa is considered a life so well lived, what should be said about the greater life of the One worshiped by her and by millions of others? We would do well to listen to His seal and verdict on the written Word.

One may, of course, ask whether the argument is not circular. We believe the Bible because Jesus affirms it to be true. We believe Jesus because the Bible says He is the Truth. The question is a fair one. But this is where the Bible stands uniquely among other religious books claiming divine authorship.

The Bible is a book whose facts can be tested outside of itself. The historical, geographical, archaeological, and prophetic data can be verified from outside the Scriptures. When sixty-six books covering a two-thousand-year span and written by approximately thirty-seven authors coalesce with such singularity, purpose, and empirical verifiability, the argument can hardly be considered circular. An honest investigation of such intricate convergences actually bespeaks a very profound moral and historical sense, dating back over four thousand years. The Bible is more than a book pointing to itself. Its attestations are multifaceted.

THE WIDE APPEAL

The second aspect of scriptural authority is revealed in its intellectual breadth. From the beginning to the end the narrative is rich in simplicity, so that even a child can grasp the truth of its stories. Yet it is so profound in its exposition of great theological themes that it has challenged the best of thinking minds and inspired the greatest of artistic genius. The stories are varied enough to apply to the king who hosted a feast; to the politician who sought the best seat in the banquet; to the athlete who ran a race; to the soldier who went to war; to the widow who lacked any income; to the shepherd who lost his sheep; to the father of a wayward son; to the fisherman who cast his nets; to the needy who longed for acceptance. In rich parable, illustration, and action Jesus spoke so that both the child and the rabbi craned their necks to hear Him.

It is very possible to miss just how meaningful is this truth. By contrast, in the religious books of another tradition a profound understanding of one particular language is necessary to even recognize the so-called miracle of the book. In the tradition of yet another, there is debate as to who is even qualified to interpret it, necessitating the birthright of a particular station in life to do so. These terribly restricting impositions do not apply to the understanding of the Scriptures. In fact, Jesus reprimanded His disciples when they discouraged children from coming to Him while fawning over those who were society's favored sons and daughters. Till this very day stories both from the Old Testament and the New Testament, such as

Solomon settling the dispute between two women who claimed to be the mother of the same child and the father waiting for the prodigal son to return, are told to eager minds, whether old or young.

It all makes sense. Why would a God who cares so particularly for the weak and disenfranchised of this world make it difficult for them to understand Him? In the middle of one of His sternest warnings to an unrepentant generation, Jesus said, "I praise you, Father, Lord of heaven and earth, because you have hidden these things from the wise and learned, and revealed them to little children. Yes, Father, for this was your good pleasure" (Matt. 11:25, 26). It is not accidental that in the darkest days of slavery in America the spirituals rang with simplicity and splendor, beckoning the slaves to steal their hearts away to Jesus or to think of that great crossing over one day into freedom and the Promised Land. Educated or uneducated, adult or child, bond or free—the Word has always been within the reach of all.

There is an important point to be made here lest a greater truth be missed. These are not just simple anecdotes or illustrations that Jesus used, not communication ploys to weave some fanciful tale. These stories, interwoven with the truths of history that narrate the very birth, life, death, and resurrection of Christ, address the existential struggle in the human heart for deliverance from the reality of evil. This method reinforces for us that the Scriptures are not inspired just in content, but also in form. Author Eugene Peterson comments on this.

> Storytelling creates a world of presuppositions, assumptions and relations into which we enter. Stories invite us into a world other than ourselves, and if they are good and true stories, a world larger than ourselves. . . . The minute we abandon the story, we reduce the reality to the dimensions of our minds and feelings and experience. . . . This is in contrast to the ancient preference for myth-making, which more or less turns us into spectators of the supernatural. It is also in contrast to the modern preference for moral philosophy which puts us in charge of our own salvation. "Gospel story" is a verbal way of accounting for reality

that, like the incarnation that is its subject, is simultaneously divine and human. It reveals, that is, it shows us something we could never come up with on our own by observation or experiment or guess, and at the same time it engages, it brings us into the action as recipients and participants but without dumping the responsibility on us for making it turn out right.[3]

Peterson goes on to point out how this form delivers us from both extremes, the one of becoming frivolous spectators always pining to be entertained by another story, the other of being anxious moralists, taking on the burdens of the world. In short, the story is more than just an illustration. It shoulders the truth of reality.

Have these not been the same extremes to which the modern mind has succumbed in facing evil? On the one hand we read story after story in the front page and succumb to becoming spectators in a journalists' arena. On the other hand we hear myriad moral philosophers offering yet another theory to address the scourge of crime. In the Scriptures there is a wholesomeness in the connecting of all of life, protecting us from a sense of entertainment when the reality should hurt and from pessimism when the hope is real. In other words, the headline story of a mother who kills her children is not lost to God in the weight of world politics and global issues. He who took pains to tell us of the sick son of a Roman soldier or of the man without sight who stationed himself at the temple in search of a cure must hurt with the things that break the heart of the individual, and He bends low not only to lift up the cause of the victim but to offer help to the victimizer.

Some of us may recall a particular author upon whom the death sentence was pronounced for "blasphemy and irreverence" shown to his religious heritage and his "holy book." Clearly the work was very disrespectful and mocking of a belief that millions held sacred. But by equal measure one must wonder about the irrationality of calling for a death sentence upon the writer. When a representative of that religion was asked on national television how such a sentence could be pronounced in disregard for the individual's right, the answer was definitive of the philosophy. "In our belief," he said, "the individual is dispensable; the cause must go on."

Here then is the cardinal difference. Jesus left the ninety-nine to search for the one, because the individual does matter. When we lose sight of people to pursue our own personal gain or when we devalue the individual in the name of cosmic priorities, we forget this truth and approach the core of evil. The Bible tells us that God knows even when a sparrow falls to the ground, that He adorns the lilies of the field, and that the very hairs of our heads are numbered. That is the degree to which His care is personal.

Jesus said, "Consider the ravens: They do not sow or reap, they have no storeroom or barn; yet God feeds them. And how much more valuable are you than birds! . . . Consider how the lilies grow. They do not labor or spin. Yet I tell you, not even Solomon in all his splendor was dressed like one of these. If that is how God clothes the grass of the field, which is here today, and tomorrow is thrown into the fire, how much more will he clothe you, O you of little faith!" (Luke 12:24, 27–28). By contrast He reminds us that "the nations are like a drop in a bucket; . . . he weighs the islands as though they were fine dust" (Isa. 40:15). The end of history will reveal the hollowness of national pursuit and the eternal value of each and every individual. History is His story told in individual hearts.

ENCOMPASSING THE WORLD

There is a third aspect of God's unique revelation in the Scriptures, the transcultural nature of His Truth. The Bible is neither Eastern nor Western but applicable to every culture, because the truth of life's purpose must always transcend any cultural shortsightedness. The imagery with which Jesus speaks so clearly addresses the Eastern mind. The parable of the ten women with their lamps waiting for the bridegroom to arrive engenders a wealth of sentiments to the Eastern reader. Anyone who has spent any time in the East can immediately envision the bridal procession, instruments playing and the accompanying throng rejoicing, making its way with the groom to the home of the bride. The whole picture is Eastern to this very day.

On the other hand, there is a touch here and there of the impact of Christ that would today be more readily identified in the West than in the East. He talks, for example, of the tyranny of the employer who lords it over the one who serves him, and He says true character is not to be found in commanding or suppressing other people but in serving one another. This reality of the dignity of labor is far more manifest in the West than it is in the East.

The impact of the gospel cannot be gainsaid on this matter. The disregard for essential human worth and the slavish pandering that is inflicted upon so much of humankind in parts of the world where the servant is considered to be inferior as a person is a terrible scourge upon people. Who we are should always be prior to what we do. Even the atheist Bertrand Russell admitted that it was debatable whether the method espoused by Mahatma Gandhi in calling for independence from the British would have succeeded except that it appealed to the conscience of a nation that had been influenced by the gospel. Today in Gandhi's ashram in the city of Ahmedabad in central India, Russell's quotation greets each visitor. How transculturally noteworthy that, in a predominantly Hindu nation, a quote by an atheist testifies to the impact of Christ upon nations both East and West, enjoining respect toward every human being.

Only in biblical terms do we see how God is able to humble each of us without humiliating us and to elevate all of us without flattering any of us. The West today lives off the capital of the Christian faith without realizing it. The work ethic of the West and the belief in the dignity of labor are biblically based. And the same equality applies in matters of race and gender, two turbulent conflicts of our time.

Peter Kreeft, professor of philosophy at Boston College, elaborates on this marvelous truth of equality that retains a difference. He demonstrates that in God's economy there is an egalitarianism in people but an elitism in ideas. By that he means the equality of all humanity but the inequality of ideas. While human beings are equal, ideas are not. By contrast, in the world's way of doing things we have created an elitism among people and an egalitarianism of ideas: We have made some people superior to others and rendered all ideas equal. The end result has been the exploitation of people and the death of truth. And that is why we have an epidemic of evil that denudes people but fights for ideas.

TRANSFORMING THE SOUL

One final argument for the authority of the Scriptures that I present is the power of this book to touch the spirit by focusing on the holiness of God rather than mandating a set of do's and don'ts as if that were at the heart of spirituality. Jesus has clearly pointed out where the root of wickedness lies.

> You have heard that it was said to the people long ago, "Do not murder, and anyone who murders will be subject to judgment." But I tell you that anyone who is angry with his brother will be subject to judgment. . . .
>
> Therefore, if you are offering your gift at the altar and there remember that your brother has something against you, leave your gift there in front of the altar. First go and be reconciled to your brother; then come and offer your gift.
>
> Settle matters quickly with your adversary. (Matt. 5:21–24)

In the same manner Jesus proceeds with the issue of lust. It was not the act of adultery alone that He spoke against, but dwelling on lustful thoughts from which adultery sprang. Does this not then address issues like pornography and violence, where thoughts sow the seeds of evil? In a similar manner He addresses the sanctity of the word, that our yes should mean yes without having to pile oath upon oath. He speaks to the terrible and unstoppable bent to exact personal revenge upon every wrong of the past. Finally Jesus climaxes that segment of His teaching by telling us that love is at the heart of all relationships and that without love, hate and anger will rule. Jesus gets to the heart—not to a set of rules that can be observed while the heart still rebels.

By setting the problem in its root form rather than in its flowering, Jesus directs us then to the holiness of God, the glimpse we need to touch our spirits. All the rules in the world cannot change a heart or make a person righteous. Only as the spirit is touched by the Spirit of God does the soul rise in worship and true goodness flow.

One of the greatest masterpieces of music composition, if not the greatest, is the work of George Frideric Handel simply called *Messiah*. Prior to its composition Handel had not been successful as a musician and had retired from much professional activity by the age of fifty-six. Then, in a remarkable series of events, a friend presented him with a libretto based on the life of Christ, the entire script of which was Scripture. Handel shut himself in his room on Brook Street in London. In twenty-four days, breathtakingly absorbed in this composition and hardly eating or drinking, Handel completed the work all the way to its orchestration. He was a man in the grip of profound inspiration. Later, as he groped for words to describe what he had experienced, he quoted Saint Paul, saying, "Whether I was in the body or out of my body when I wrote it I know not."[4] Handel's servant testified that on one occasion when he walked into the room to plead with him to eat, he saw Handel with tears streaming down his face saying, "I did think I did see all Heaven before me, and the great God Himself."[5]

When *Messiah* was staged in London, as the notes of the Hallelujah Chorus rang out—"King of Kings and Lord of Lords. . . . And

He shall reign forever and ever"—the king of England, drawn irresistibly, stood to his feet, and the audience followed as one.

Listen to how one writer sums up the impact of *Messiah*:

> Handel personally conducted more than thirty performances of *Messiah*, many of these concerts were for the benefit of the hurting and the needy. "*Messiah* has fed the hungry, clothed the naked, fostered the orphan. . . ." Another wrote, "Perhaps the works of no other composer have so largely contributed to the relief of human suffering." Still another said, "*Messiah's* music has done more to convince thousands of mankind that there is a God about us than all the theological works ever written."[6]

Even if overstated, the point is well taken. The work was based entirely on Scripture. The focus was on the person of Christ. The spirit of a man was enraptured by the holiness of God. A king rose spontaneously to his feet. The people followed his example. The first performance was a charitable benefit to raise money to free 142 people from prison who could not pay their debts. In the prison of suffering and evil within which the whole world now lives, the same Messiah offers us deliverance.

Young Ashley Oubré, is right. Her future, Western civilization's future, and indeed, the world's future, will depend on the answer to her question. Will we restore to the Bible its rightful authority or leave it for young minds till they can grow into our evil-ridden world? Only that which is ineradicable and true can counter that which must be eradicated and false. This preeminent role against the false ideas that are the root cause of evil is that of the Scriptures.

The Inextinguishable Light

IN THE FIRST SECTION of this book I commented that the basis upon which secularism attacked religious knowledge would ultimately destroy not just belief in God but belief in the very concept of truth itself. That is the deduction I will presently sustain. If this conflct is not resolved, nothing else will matter, for nothing will make sense. On this issue the two foundations of secularism and Christianity differ. Once this is settled, the answers we seek may be found.

THE COLLAPSE OF A CATEGORY

The much-heralded belief of the postmodern West is that skepticism on ultimate matters is the law by which we must live. Truth as a category in relation to metaphysical issues no longer exists. All is relative. This surrender of truth is the hallmark of our culture's greatest crisis and makes the culture war so deadly, restricting meaningful dialogue on questions of the soul.

Winston Churchill once said that the most valuable thing in the world is the truth. So valuable is it, said he, that it needs to be constantly protected by a bodyguard of lies. Churchill made that remark in the context of intelligence and counterintelligence efforts during the Second World War. This assertion from that great statesman was probably the only pronouncement on which he and his nemesis, Adolf Hitler, agreed.

Unfortunately, the propagation of lies is not restricted to conventional military warfare—it has also been the most insidious weapon in the war of ideas. And what is more, the practice of lying, according to surveys, is at epidemic proportions—assuming, of course, that those surveyed told the truth!

All that aside, as valuable a commodity as it is and as indispensable as it is to meaningful existence, truth is possibly the most violated concept in our world. This is more so now than ever before in history. The lies that punctuate business transactions, the lies by which trusted relationships have been destroyed—these we are aware of. The greater tragedy is not just that we live with a proliferation of lies but that this is probably the first time, certainly in Western civilization, that society at large does not believe in the existence of absolute truth.

Such radical step toward moral and metaphysical skepticism, which asserts the very impossibility of knowing the laws by which our individual lives must be governed, is the single greatest indicator of our postmodern mind. What is most surprising is that a posture of disbelief in truth is not restricted to the liberal element; instead, truth as a category has been jettisoned by many at all levels of society, even among conservatives.

According to a study reported by George Barna in 1991, 67 percent of the U.S. population did not believe in absolute truth. In 1994, that figure rose to 75 percent. In 1991, 52 percent of evangelicals did not believe in absolute truth. In 1994, that figure rose to 62 percent. The difference between saying there is no such thing as the truth and living as if truth does not matter is a small one, and the consequences for both are catastrophic.

THE PERNICIOUSNESS OF ITS EFFECT

Several decades ago Malcolm Muggeridge warned of this spiritual plague coming upon the West, branding it her ultimate death wish. In his autobiography he beckoned humanity to beware of this, the most destructive of all trends—the death of truth. This is how he worded it:

> Yet even so, truth is very beautiful: more so I consider than justice—today's pursuit which easily puts on a false face. In the nearly seven decades I have lived through, the world has overflowed with bloodshed and explosions whose dust has never had time to settle before others have erupted. All in purportedly just causes. . . . The lies on behalf of which our wars have been fought and our peace treaties concluded! The lies of revolution and of counter-revolution! The lies of advertising, of news, of salesmanship, of politics! The lies of the priest in his pulpit, the professor at his podium, the journalist at his typewriter! The lie stuck like a fishbone in the throat of the microphone, the hand-held lies of the prowling cameraman! Ignazio Silone told me once how when he was a member of the Old Comintern, some stratagem was under discussion, and a delegate, a newcomer who had never attended before, made the extraordinary observation that if such and such a statement were to be made, it wouldn't be true. There was a moment of dazed silence, and then everyone began to laugh. They laughed and laughed till tears ran down their cheeks, and the Kremlin walls began to shake. The same laughter echoes in every Council chamber and cabinet room. Wherever two or more are gathered to exercise authority, it is truth that has died, not God.[1]

The most disconcerting aspect of this attitude toward truth is that anyone who holds to the possibility of truth is categorized as one who merely "believes" that truth exists. The implication is that because truth does not exist, what is held to be true is only a belief and is therefore not a rationally admissible fact. At the same time, those who dismiss truth can end up believing anything at all, and any belief that is contemptuous of truth is considered plausible for that reason alone. This is the raw nerve of postmodern existence, and unless we establish the possibility and the necessity of truth and of how one arrives at the truth, any belief system can be mocked at will or offhandedly dismissed as cultural.

For the Christian this is where the battle must be fought, for no world-view suffers more from the loss of truth than the Christian one. Strangely, as has been noted, other religions are culturally protected; no one had dare make light of an Eastern religious belief. The Christian faith, however, is free game for ridicule and analysis by social critics and is afforded no protection from hate or hostility by our so-called multicultural society. In a culture where truth no longer exists, the very cardinal statement of Jesus, "I am the way and the truth and the life," becomes meaningless. And unless truth as a category is defended every commitment that is made because of a commitment to Christ Himself will be deemed a "mere belief" and differentiated from fact, thereby making it unworthy of intellectual assent.

THE DAWNING OF AN ERA

Scholars who deal in social theory and cultural shifts tell us that the modern world as we know it spanned the two hundred years from 1789 to 1989—from the storming of the Bastille in France, which signaled the beginning of the French Revolution, to the dismantling of the Berlin Wall, which symbolized the collapse of communism. That brought the modern era to an end and ushered in the postmodern world. But the breakdown of both these edifices of human construction, with all the tyranny they represented, is meager compared to the breakdown now facing the West, a breakdown heartily sanctioned by the free Western societies now basking under the banner of the postmodern mind. In the modern world reason reigned supreme, and it was envisioned that rational man would hold all things together. Now, *postmodernism* has become the buzzword in academia, the word by which all things have fallen apart, for reason itself is banished as a dinosaur in humanity's evolutionary climb, and truth is considered extinct.

The modern world had emphasized purpose and design. The postmodern world emphasizes randomness and chance. The modern world sought stability in values. The postmodern world sees values as transient and relative. The modern world saw reason as the means and meaning as the end. The postmodern world glories in unreason and celebrates meaninglessness. The modern world pursued a synthesis of all disciplines in its search to find the unity of truth. The postmodern world focuses on deconstruction and extols the marvel of contradiction. In short, the very purpose of the university, which was to find unity in diversity, is now in contradiction to its own name, and students are graduating unable to bridge the disciplines and proudly boasting a skepticism that one can be sure of anything.

This is the one monumental difference between the modern and the postmodern mind. In the modern pursuit, even though there was an inhospitable climate toward spiritual truths, debate was nevertheless possible because information was still subject to induction and deduction. Calm spirits could prevail to allow facts a place in dialogue. In the postmodernist mentality the purpose of dialogue or debate is not for truth but only for feeling, and as passion has taken over, facts are given no legitimacy. The result is hate-filled shouting matches.

If any progress is to be made amid the shifting sands of cultural change it is imperative that we understand where any meaningful dialogue can begin. Too much is at stake, and too many lives will be hurt or lost if we are unable to agree even on the starting point.

This is not to imply that a moral consensus can be reached purely by arriving at the truth. Not by any means. But it does assert that at least in theory we can determine whether a statement that is made about reality is true or false. If even that is denied, then no judgment on any statement is possible. That state of affairs is rationally inadmissable and existentially unlivable.

THE SEDUCTION OF A LIE

We recall Aristotle's reminder that truth is primary, from which morality and technique flow. In our time, technology is supreme, morality is mocked, and truth has been eradicated. But thankfully, all is not lost, for at least postmodernism has unwittingly awakened society to the realization that truth, morality, and meaning are connected. If the first goes, there is nothing on which to base the other two. On every side society feels this colossal breakdown, and a stirring is taking place deep within the national conscience that when truth has been lost, the results are devastating. Nowhere has this been felt more than among those who think in the area of morality and ethics within the legal system and by our young people whose lives reflect the turmoil and emptiness within.

Consequently, many are aroused from their stupor, a stupor that the modern mind created when it trumpeted that rational man could arrive at his Utopia without God's absolutes. In fact, so drastic has been the realization that our purpose on earth is inextricably bound to our behavior that some scholars are reluctantly admitting that the teaching of the Bible provided a logical basis for goodness and that with the abandonment of the Judeo-Christian ethic, the basis for morality is gone. So how do such antagonists to the gospel message then deal with this need for a foundational ethic?

The suggestions range from the absurd to the preposterous. Take, for example, one scholar who presented his thesis at a 1991 symposium of the American Association for the Advancement of Science in Washington, D.C. His basic argument began with the admission that a catastrophe has come upon us as a people. Philosopher Loyal Rue argued that science has made it impossible to believe any longer in the myths of the Bible, myths such as God giving the Ten Commandments and Jesus rising from the dead. But with the loss of these tenets, he said, we have lost the very underpinnings of moral theory that had provided a legitimate recognition of accountability and charity. We are left, therefore, with the unprecedented situation of needing to concoct a "noble lie" so powerful that it will furnish us with reasons to be good, even though those reasons in themselves will be untrue. This is how he worded it:

> The illusion must be so imaginative and so compelling that it can't be resisted. What I mean by the noble lie is one that deceives us, tricks us, compels us beyond self interest, beyond ego . . . that will deceive us into the view that our moral discourse must serve the interests not only of ourselves and each other, but those of the earth as well.[2]

One should rightly be incredulous at the extent to which some will wantonly and deliberately dupe themselves. But let us take a beneficent route, because here again, there is a tacit concession that a purpose to life and a sense of accountability to a higher moral law are inseparably connected to the justification of ethics. In effect, what is being said here is that without a transcendent order, ethics is unjustifiable, and without ethics, life is unlivable.

On all fronts, therefore, our existential realities are pointing us to the relationship between truth and life. And what reality has revealed to be joined together, let no man put asunder. In short, the greatest concern of our time should be the recovery of truth. It was not too long ago that in a survey among Canadian young people, the majority said their greatest longing in life was to find someone they could believe in. The question is, how do we arrive at the truth, principally the truth on which all other truths hang and by which life must be governed?

The irony of defining truth is that while in practice we all instinctively recognize it when we see it, we nevertheless ask whether it exists theoretically. Professor Dallas Willard, who teaches philosophy at the University of Southern California, asks this of our sensitivity to and estrangement from the truth. What would you think if you asked your ten-year-old, "Susie, did you eat the cookies on the counter?" and she placidly replied, "Mother, what is truth?" Thankfully, Susie may not have gained that evasive philosophical sophistication. But Pilate of old had, and he raised the question of Jesus, "What is truth?" Jesus answered him with a categorical response (see John 18:38). But before we turn to His answer, let us establish some definitions.

First, we know that relativism as a theory cannot be true. The Greek philosopher Protagoras was the one who said, "The human being is the measure of all things." By that he meant that each individual measured in terms for himself or herself the fact or nature of anything. He was disagreeing with Parmenides, who stated that what is, is; what is not, is not. Without getting too far afield it would be simplest to demonstrate the fairly obvious that Protagoras's relativism is self-defeating. Professor Allen Wood of Yale University states it succinctly:

> The problem arises as soon as Protagoras tries either to *assert* relativism or to *believe* it. To assert a proposition is to say that it is true (and its denial false). To believe a proposition is to believe it is true (and its denial false). Thus if Protagoras asserts relativism, then he asserts that relativism is true, and that those (such as Plato) who deny relativism say and believe something false. But relativism denies that anyone can say or believe anything false. Hence to be consistent Protagoras must concede that the denier of relativism says and believes something true. Consequently relativism is committed to saying that its own denial is true, and in this refutes itself.[3]

THE SCAFFOLDING OF CERTAINTY

Very simply stated, truth is the judgment expressed when we use the word "is." The verb "is" asserts something about reality to which the statement conforms. In other words, the statement "This is so" expresses a state of existence that is real and not dependent on someone's belief in it to make it true. The reality being represented is objective, universal, and transcendent. This is precisely the logic by which we operate and the logic by which we either make statements about reality or make denials about what is not real.

It is of supreme importance to know that, as Mortimer Adler has said:

> The logic of truth is the same for all exclusionary claims to truth. Any claims that are correctly judged to be true also imply that all judgments to the contrary are false. The proposition may be a theorem in mathematics, a scientific generalization, a conclusion of historic research, a philosophical principle, or an article of faith.[4]

This leads us to the definition of an *absolute*. An absolute is basically an unchanging point of reference by which all other changes are measured. Each discipline brings with it a handful of certainties by which others are developed. Those certainties, if assumed, must be previously demonstrated when used as absolutes. In contrast, relativism in ethics denounces absolutes and erects an indefensible system that leaves all morality at the mercy of individual whim. *Relativism* is, therefore, only another word for *anarchy*, and that is why truth itself becomes elusive when there is no longer a point of reference.

Where, then, may one begin? There are fundamentally four questions that every thinking human being must answer: the questions of origin, meaning, morality, and destiny. How did life come to be in the first place? To what purpose is my life? How may I choose between right and wrong? What happens to me when I die? When these questions are individually answered, the answers must be seen to correspond with reality. These answers are then collectively tested for coherence, that is, that they do not contradict each other. Answers that correspond with reality and fit into a coherent system provide the individual a world-view by which all of life's choices may then be made.

For the Christian, the starting point is God. *He* is the eternally existent one, the absolute, from whom we draw all definitions for life's purpose and destiny. This God does not expect us to come to Him in a vacuum. He has so framed this world and our minds that the laws of reason and logic we use lead us to the certainty of His being and assure us that we may know Him who is the source of all truth. At this point the argument is a bit rigorous, but it is vitally important. Philosopher Norman Geisler says, "In order of being God is first: but in order of knowing, logic leads us to all knowledge of God. God is the basis of all logic (in order of being), but logic is the basis of all knowledge of God (in order of knowing)."[5] If one finds this statement too rigid, let us present it in a softer version. The right process of reasoning must at some point be invoked in order to defend the reality and "knowability" of God.

THE STRUCTURE OF REASON

Here we run aground and face the first criticism from the skeptic: Are we not using logic with which to prove logic? The answer to that is straightforward. The logical system is built on four fundamental laws, laws that are impossible to argue against without at the same time proving them. For the sake of brevity, let me discuss just two of them.

First is the Law of Noncontradiction. This law affirms that no two contradictory statements can be both true and false at the same time in the same sense. To deny the Law of Noncontradiction is only to affirm it, for to say that the Law of Noncontradiction is not true is to assume that the denial is true and the law is not. But that is precisely what the law says—that two contradictory statements cannot both be true. There is no way to get around this.

The second foundational law is the Law of Rational Inference. By that we mean that inferences can be made from what is known to what is unknown. No one can prove any point without the Law of

Rational Inference. There are conclusions that may be legitimately drawn when statements are true and the argument containing those statements is valid.

Postmodern skeptics cannot tolerate the Law of Noncontradiction because of the rational inferences they draw from it—that truth does exist—but it is evident that they live by the implications of these laws. And what is more, one of the most fallacious ideas ever spawned in Western attitudes toward truth is the oft-repeated pronouncement that exclusionary claims to truth are a Western way of thinking. The East, it is implied, is all-inclusionary. This is patently false. Every religion, without exception, has some foundational beliefs that are categorically nonnegotiable and exclude everything to the contrary.

Truth by definition is exclusive. If truth were all-inclusive, nothing would be false. And if nothing were false, what would be the meaning of truth? Furthermore, if nothing were false, would it be true to say that everything is false? It quickly becomes evident that nonsense would follow. In short, therefore, truth boils down to two tests: Statements must correspond to reality, and any system of thought that is developed as a result must be coherent. The correspondence and coherence tests are applied by all of us in matters that affect us.

Therefore, when Jesus said, "I am the way and the truth and the life. No man comes to the father except through me," He was making a very reasonable statement by affirming truth's exclusivity. The question one may legitimately ask is whether He demonstrated that claim rather than just stating it.

THE BATTLEGROUND OF THE HEART

Let us see, now, how Jesus responded to Pilate's question. The conversation had begun with Pilate asking Jesus if, indeed, He was a king. The very surprising answer of Jesus was, "Is that your idea, or did others talk to you about me?" (John 18:34).

This is the first and most important step to understanding the nature of truth. In effect, Jesus was asking Pilate if this was a genuine question or purely an academic one. He was not merely checking on Pilate's sincerity. He was opening up Pilate's heart to himself to reveal to Pilate his unwillingness to deal with the implications of Jesus' answer. Intent in the pursuit of truth is prior to content or to the availability of it. Author George MacDonald once said, "To give truth to him who loves it not is only to give him more plentiful reasons for misinterpretation."[6] The love of truth and the willingness to submit to its demands is the first step.

But Jesus said something else that is even more extraordinary. After identifying His Lordship in a kingdom that was not of this world, He said, "Everyone on the side of truth *listens to me*" (John 18:37, italics mine). Jesus was not merely establishing the existence of truth but His pristine embodiment of it. He was *identical* to the truth. This meant that everything He said and did, and the life He lived in the flesh, represented that which was in keeping with ultimate reality. Therefore, to reject Him is to choose to govern oneself with a lie.

THE WORD AS TRUTH

Let me take this point further. In the beginning, when God created the heavens and the earth, He branded His creation "good." That word both defined reality and specified how we ought to live. Out of that relationship with God, all other relationships take their cue, including the use of language in defining the world. We read that Adam named the creatures. That naming was the work of man as sub-sovereign, defining reality in God's terms.

It was at this point that truth was tested. The temptation of Satan was the challenge to the first humans to take upon themselves the prerogative of God and redefine reality in their own terms. The lie entered, and truth was violated by rejecting the propositional revelation of God and contradicting His definitions of good and evil. By yielding to that temptation Adam and Eve "exchanged the truth of God for a lie" and chose to create their own realities. This, as God had warned, led to death and destruction.

It is noteworthy that when the tempter came to Jesus in the wilderness the temptation was the same, namely, to make His own terms for living. Jesus rejected this seduction by quoting the Word, i.e., the definitions of God. As mentioned earlier, it is interesting that Jesus quoted from the Book of Deuteronomy, which literally means the "second law." This was God's law reiterated to His people—not as heteronomy, with the state as the authority; not as an undefined theonomy, with intuition or culture as the authority; and not as autonomy with self as the authority. This was God's law as given in the beginning, and it represented the nature of reality as God had designed it. The opposite of Deuteronomy is autonomy, or self law. It is in this context that we must understand Jesus' statement that the truthfulness of one's intent is revealed by the response to Him, for He is the fulfillment of God's law and the expression of His truth.

THE EMPIRICAL DEMONSTRATION

God's answers to the four basic questions, however, are not just proven by the process of abstract reasoning but are also sustained by the rigors of experience. And in the reality of history, He has demonstrated empirically the living out of truth in the birth, life, death, and resurrection of His Son.

In short, the intimations of truth come in multisensory fashion. The Guardian of Reason leads us to check the correspondence of His word with reality and ascertain the coherence of the assertions. Our grand privilege is to know Him, to bring our lives into conformity with truth that leads us to that coherence within. He has said, "If you hold to my teaching, you are really my disciples. Then you will know the truth, and the truth will set you free" (John 8:31, 32). In a world increasingly enslaved by error and alienation, how wonderful to be freed by the truth to His peace. The Scriptures tell us that the enemy of our souls is the father of all lies. He will do anything to keep us from coming to the truth, because it is the most valuable thing in the world and leads us to the source of all truth, to God Himself.

SKEPTICISM'S SURRENDER

To all of this the skeptic might say that such conclusions may be drawn only if the God of the Bible exists. To that I heartily answer, *Absolutely!* And on numerous campuses around the world it has been my thrilling privilege to present a defense for the existence of God and for the authority of the Scriptures, unique in their splendor and convincing in the truth they proclaim. But let us not miss what the skeptic unwittingly surrenders by saying that all this could be true only if God exists. For, implicit in that concession is the application of the Law of Noncontradiction and the Law of Rational Inference, which exist only if truth exists. Truth, in turn, can exist only if there is an objective standard by which to measure it. That objective, unchanging absolute is God.

I heard a cute little story, growing up in India. It is the story of a little boy who had lots of pretty marbles. But he was constantly eyeing his sister's bagful of candy. One day he said to her, "If you give me all your candy, I'll give you all of my marbles." She gave it much thought and agreed to the trade. He took all her candy and went back to his room to get his marbles. But the more he eyed them the more reluctant he became to give them all up. So he hid the best of them under his pillow and took the rest to her. That night she slept soundly while he tossed and turned restlessly, unable to sleep and thinking, *I wonder if she gave me all the candy.*

I have often wondered, when I see our angry culture claiming that

God has not given us enough evidence, if it is not the veiled restlessness of lives lived in doubt because of their own duplicity. God calls us all to enjoy His glorious truth. We believe, but not because we need to in order to make us feel better. We believe because truth survives in the end and it is truth that must be believed. What is more, when we trust Him who is the source of all truth there is an enjoyment in life beyond any momentary pleasure a lie can give. The battle in our time is posed as one of the intellect in the assertion that truth is unknowable. But that may be only a veneer for the real battle, that of the heart.

Annotated Bibliography on the Bible

Comfort, Philip Wesley, ed. *The Origin of the Bible*. Wheaton, Ill.: Tyndale House, 1992. Noted biblical scholars address the inspiration, translation and manuscripts of the Old and New Testaments, as well as the development of the canon. F. F. Bruce, Carl Henry, and R. K. Harrison are among the contributing authors.

Geisler, Norman. *Christian Apologetics*. Grand Rapids, Mich.: Baker, 1976. The classic resource on various tests for truth (such as rationalism and agnosticism) and world-views. The final section of the book examines the historical reliability of the New Testament and the case for the authority and inspiration of the Bible.

Geisler, Norman, ed. *Inerrancy*. Grand Rapids, Mich.: Zondervan, 1979. This book is a compendium of the scholarly papers presented at the International Conference on Biblical Inerrancy in 1978. J. Barton Payne's chapter on "Higher Criticism and Biblical Inerrancy" is an excellent examination of higher criticism's presuppositions and its unscientific disregard for the scriptures under observation.

Geisler, Norman, and William E. Nix. *From God to Us: How We Got Our Bible*. Chicago: Moody, 1974. A basic but thorough primer on the Bible's origins, including consideration of manuscripts, textual criticism, and early translations. Especially insightful are their discussions of what qualifies a book's authenticity and of the development of the Old Testament canon.

Habermas, Gary R. *Ancient Evidence for the Life of Jesus: Historical Records of His Death and Resurrection*. Nashville: Thomas Nelson, 1984. The author addresses the many extrabiblical sources—both Christian and non-Christian—and archaeological evidence that offer information on the life, death, and resurrection of Jesus. The initial chapters on historical methodology present a philosophy of history (how one studies a particular event) and the procedure of historical investigation.

Montgomery, John Warwick, ed. *God's Inerrant Word: An International Symposium on the Trustworthiness of the Scriptures.* Minneapolis: Bethany, 1974. A compendium of the papers given at the Conference on the Inspiration and Authority of the Scriptures in 1973. Scholars offering research articles include theologians J. I. Packer and John Gerstner, and philosopher John Frame.

Moreland, J.P. *Scaling the Secular City: A Defense of Christianity.* Grand Rapids, Mich.: Baker, 1987. Moreland provides an astute critique of secularism and communicates the rationality of Christianity. His scholarship reveals secularism's inadequacy in offering the individual meaning to live and reasons for being moral. His second chapter on the historicity of the New Testament and the resurrection of Jesus are concisely yet persuasively presented.

Wilkins, Michael J., and J. P. Moreland, eds. *Jesus Under Fire: Modern Scholarship Reinvents the Historical Jesus.* Grand Rapids, Mich.: Zondervan, 1995. New Testament scholars and philosophers examine the claims and methodology of the Jesus Seminar and present a well-argued case for the orthodox understanding of Jesus. The criticism regarding exclusivism and pluralism is also countered.

Wright, N. T. *Who Was Jesus?* Grand Rapids, Mich.: Eerdmans, 1993. An English scholar responds to the latest controversial works on the life of Jesus by Barbara Thiering, John Shelby Spong, and others. Wright offers an excellent overview of the broad arguments of this debate.

Notes

INTRODUCTION

1 George Santayana, "The Life of Reason," *Who Said What When* (London: Bloomsbury Publishing, 1989), 211.

CHAPTER I   *The Winds of Change*

1 I use the terms *soul* and *spirit* interchangeably here, not to provide a theological framework, but to refer to the essence of each and every person as not merely material in being and bound to earthliness but as fashioned by our Creator to think His thoughts after Him, to rise beyond the physical, and to understand the purpose of our being in this world.

2 Jay Parini, "Academic Conservatives Who Decry Politicization Show Staggering Naiveté about Their Own Biases," *Chronicle of Higher Education*, 7 December 1988, B-1.

3 Dinesh D'Souza is a research fellow at the American Enterprise Institute.

4 Myron Magnet is an editor of *Fortune* magazine and a fellow of the Manhattan Institute.

5 Norman Mailer, "The White Negro," 1957. Quoted by Myron Magnet in *The Dream and the Nightmare: The Sixties' Legacy to the Underclass* (New York: William Morrow, 1993), 35.

6   Katherine Lee Bates, "America the Beautiful."

CHAPTER 2   *Dying Beliefs and Stillborn Hopes*

1   Arthur Guiterman, "Gaily the Troubadour," from *Gaily the Troubadour* (New York: E.P. Dutton & Company, Inc., 1936).
2   Peter L. Berger, *The Sacred Canopy*, (New York: Doubleday, 1990) 107.

CHAPTER 3   *The High Noon of Promise*

1   Julian Marias, *America in the Fifties and Sixties*, edited by Aaron Rockland (University Park, Penna: Pennsylvania State University Press, 1972), 412.
2   Russell Kirk, *The Roots of American Order* (Malibu, Calif.: Pepperdine University Press, 1978), 467, emphasis mine.
3   William Blake, from "Milton," *The Portable Romantic Poets: Blake to Poe*, ed. William Auden and Norman Holmes Pearson (New York: Penguin, 1987), 24.
4   John Warwick Montgomery, *The Shaping of America* (Minneapolis: Bethany Fellowship, 1976), 73.
5   Russell Kirk, *The Roots of American Order*, 93–94.
6   G. K. Chesterton, "A Hymn," in *As I Was Saying*, ed. Robert Knille (Grand Rapids, Mich.: Eerdman's, 1984), 27. Set to the tune of "The Church's One Foundation." Used by permission of A.P. Watt Ltd, London, on behalf of the Royal Literary Fund.
7   William Wordsworth, "London 1802," *English Romantic Writers*, ed. David Perkins (New York, Chicago, San Francisco: Harcourt, Brace & World, 1967), 288.
8   George F. Will has written a book coining these words, titled *Statecraft as Soulcraft* (New York: Simon & Schuster, 1983).

CHAPTER 4   *The Storms of Conflict*

1   Thomas C. Arthur, "Death of Another Salesman," Copyright 1961 Christian Century Foundation. Reprinted by permission from the February 1, 1961 issue of the *Christian Century*.
2   Arthur Leonard Griffith, *God's Time and Ours* (New York: Abingdon Press, 1964), 83.
3   Kenneth L. Woodward, "Religion: God Gets the He-Ho," *Newsweek*, 11 September 1995, © 1955, Newsweek Inc. All rights reserved. Reprinted by permission.
4   Predictably, secularism as a social theory did not stop at merely attacking biblical truth; it has ended up attacking the notion of truth itself. Please see the discussion on this in Appendix B.

CHAPTER 5   *The Twilight of Decency*

1   C. S. Lewis, *The Pilgrim's Regress* (Glasgow: William Collins & Sons, Fount Paperbacks, 1933), 82–83.

2   Scanner theory is described by M. Scott Peck in *A World Waiting to Be Born* (New York: Bantam, 1993), 10.
3   C. S. Lewis, *The Great Divorce* (Glasgow: William Collins & Sons, 1946), 57.
4   See Gen. 4:9–12.

CHAPTER 6   *With Deference for Difference*

1   Malvina Reynolds, "Little Boxes," words and music by Malvina Reynolds © copyright 1962, Schroder Music Co. (ASCAP), Renewed 1990. Used by permission. All rights reserved.
2   Carly Simon, "Playing Possum." Copyright by C'est Music (ASCAP.) Used by permission.
3   Vivekananda, as reported by the *Chicago Tribune*, 20 September 1893, quoted by David L. Johnson, *A Reasoned Look at Asian Religions* (Minneapolis: Bethany, 1985), 106.
4   Jack Miles, "Black vs. Browns," *Atlantic Monthly*, October 1992, 41.
5   James Davison Hunter, *Culture Wars* (New York: Basic Books, 1991), 69–70.
6   Will Herberg, cited in Hunter, *Culture Wars*.
7   Although statistics show a rapid increase in the number of Muslims to the point of becoming the second largest religion in the world and in the United States by the year 2000, one should be careful how to read these numbers. For example, numerical computation for Islam cannot be considered to have been done with the same methodology as for the Christian community. In many Islamic countries it is illegal to convert from Islam to another faith, and where it is not illegal, it is certainly a life-threatening situation. This point is often forgotten by Muslims themselves when presenting their "growth." It would be fascinating to see what would happen if the compulsive hand of law and government in enforcing religion were removed. The whole teaching of Islam in its inception rested upon the creation of an identity of a people in contradistinction to Judaism and Christianity. A failure to understand the implications of all this leads to enormous misunderstandings when all religions are grouped together.
8   Michel Guillaume Jean de Crevecoeur, quoted in Arthur Schlesinger, "The Disuniting of America," *American Educator*, Winter 1991, 14.
9   Malcolm Muggeridge, *The End of Christendom* (Grand Rapids, Mich.: Eerdmans, 1980), 52–53. Used by permission.

CHAPTER 7   *The Flickering Flame of Reason*

1   Pantheism, that strand of Hinduism that identifies God and nature as one, is ultimately handcuffed on the fundamental question of the origin and destiny of evil. If everything is divine, where does wickedness come from? As philosopher Norm Geisler says in his book *Christian Apologetics*, "The ship of pantheism is wrecked on the reef of evil" (Grand Rapids, Mich.: Baker, 1976), 189.
2   G. K. Chesterton, *Orthodoxy* (Garden City, N.Y.: Doubleday, 1959), 41.
3   Daniel Yankelovich, "New Rules in American Life: Searching for Self-fulfillment in a World Turned Upside Down," *Psychology Today*, April 1981, 36.

4   Ibid., 50.

5   Ibid.

6   Ulysses, in William Shakespeare's *Troilus and Cressida*, 3, 3, 120ff.

CHAPTER 8   *The Disoriented Self*

1   Quoted by F. W. Boreham in "An Epic of Concentration," *A Late Lark Singing* (London: Epworth Press, 1945), 128.

2   Ibid.

3   Ibid., 129.

4   Robert Shapiro, in a transcript of a CNN interview with Larry King, 2 April 1996, 5.

5   Justin Hayward, "Question," © copyright 1970 Tyler Music Ltd., London, England. Essex Music International, Inc., New York. Used by permission.

CHAPTER 9   *Establishing Boundaries*

1   Samuel Taylor Coleridge, quoted in *The International Dictionary of Thoughts*, comp. John P. Bradley, Leo F. Daniels, and Thomas C. Jones (Chicago: J. G. Ferguson, 1969), 362.

2   G. K. Chesterton, quoted in John Bartlett, *Bartlett's Familiar Quotations*, 14th ed. (Boston, Toronto: Little, Brown, 1968), 918.

3   Percy Bysshe Shelley, "Ozymandias," taken from *English Romantic Writers*, ed. David Perkins (New York, Chicago, San Francisco, Atlanta: Harcourt, Brace & World, 1967), 971.

4   James Russell Lowell, "Once to Every Man and Nation."

CHAPTER 10   *Pulling Down the Fences*

1   John Adams, *A Biography in His Own Words*, ed. James Bishop Peabody (New York: Newsweek, 1973), 121–22.

2   Malcolm Muggeridge in a verbal communication.

3   Alfred Edersheim, *Old Testament Bible History* (Wilmington, Dela.: Associated Publishers and Authors, n.d.), 556.

4   Peggy Noonan, "You'd Cry Too If It Happened to You," *FORBES*, 14 September, 1992, 69. Reprinted by permission of *FORBES* Magazine © Forbes Inc., 1992.

5   Os Guinness, *The American Hour* (New York: The Free Press, 1993), 29.

6   Cunningham Geikie, *Hours with the Bible: Manasseh to Zedekiah* (New York: John B. Alden, 1887), 25–26.

7   James Russell Lowell, "The Present Crisis."

8   The source of all these statistics is Carol Bellamy, executive director, United Nations Children's Fund, UNICEF, *The State of the World's Children* (published for UNICEF by Oxford University Press, 1996).

9   Quoted in Bellamy, *The State of the World's Children*, 1996.

10   Arthur Schlesinger Jr., "The Opening of the American Mind," *The New York Times Book Review*, July 23 1989, 27. Used by permission.

1   2 Kings 23:25
2   From Lady Margaret Thatcher's address to the Church of Scotland, 21 May 1988. Permission granted by the office of Baroness Thatcher, London.
3   Taken from a list of quotations on the back cover of a book.
4   G. K. Chesterton, "In Defense of Nonsense," 1911, quoted in Bartlett, *Bartlett's Familiar Quotations*, 918.
5   Horatio G. Spafford, "It Is Well With My Soul."
6   George MacDonald, *Life Essential: The Hope of the Gospel* (Wheaton, Ill.: Harold Shaw Publishers, 1974) quoted in Philip Yancy, *The Jesus I Never Knew* (Grand Rapids, Mich.: Zondervan, 1995), 77.
7   Malcolm Muggeridge, *The End of Christendom*, 49–50.

1   Ron Rosenbaum, "The Devil in Long Island," *New York Times Magazine*, 22 August 1993, 21–27, 36–38, 42–44.
2   Ibid., 44.
3   Ron Rosenbaum, "Staring into the Heart of Darkness: Evil Is Back," *New York Times Magazine*, 4 June 1995, 36–72.
4   Ibid., 41.
5   Hannah Arendt, *Eichmann in Jerusalem* (New York: Viking Penguin, 1977), 252, emphasis is mine.
6   The *Pulp Fiction* dialogue is from Ron Rosenbaum, "Staring into the Heart of Darkness: Evil Is Back," 44.
7   C. S. Lewis, *The Abolition of Man* (New York: Macmillan, 1947), 35.
8   This is not to deny some emotional disorders where there is emotional numbing, a psychological condition. This is only to state that a person who lives by the rule that all morality is only individual preference will ultimately breed either a heartless philosophy or a heartless life.
9   Reprinted with the permission of Simon & Schuster from *Letters and Papers from Prison:* revised, enlarged edition by Dietrich Bonhoeffer. Translated by Reginald Fuller, Frank Clark et al. Copyright © 1953, 1967, 1971 by SCM Press, Ltd.

1   Charles Wesley, "And Can It Be."
2   R. S. Thomas, "The Coming" *The Later Poems of R. S. Thomas, 1972–1982* (London: Macmillan, nd.) Used by permission of Paper Mac, London.
3   William Cowper, "God Moves in a Mysterious Way."
4   Hermann Hagedorn, *The Bomb That Fell on America*, new rev. ed. (New York: Association Press, 1950).

APPENDIX A   *The Ineradicable Word*

1   Ashley Danielle Oubré. Used by permission.

2   An annotated bibliography dealing with this subject follows this Appendix. As demeaning as the comment may seem, it must be said that some recent attacks on the historicity of the New Testament by radical scholars from groups such as the Jesus Seminar are so prejudicial and bizarre that even noted liberal scholars have rejected their ill-founded deductions. Such absurdity notwithstanding, these attacks have nevertheless been responded to by conservative scholars. If the defense of the Scriptures were made on such sparse accumulation of evidence as that upon which these extreme views have been constructed, the proponents of those theories would have scornfully dismissed such defense as unworthy of any response. But a tabloid mentality prevails in these matters even in respected journals, and even the most aberrant thesis gains legitimacy when a doctoral degree after the author's name is placed in the byline. There is no other explanation for the credulity of such intellectuals other than that they want to believe the spurious and desire to be so duped.

3   Eugene H. Peterson, *Subversive Christianity* (Vancouver: Regent College Bookstore, 1994), 4–5.

4   Patrick Kavanaugh, *The Spiritual Lives of Great Composers* (Nashville: Sparrow Press, 1992), 5.

5   Hertha Pauli, *Handel and the Messiah Story* (New York: Meredith, 1968), 51.

6   Kavanaugh, 6.

APPENDIX B   *The Inextinguishable Light*

1   Malcolm Muggeridge, *The Green Stick* (New York: William Morrow, 1973), 19.

2   George Cornell, "Religion and Ethics," *Houston Post*, 7 July 1991.

3   Professor Allen Wood, Cornell University philosophy class lecture notes, 1993.

4   Mortimer Adler, *Truth in Religion* (New York: Macmillan, 1990), 10.

5   Norman L. Geisler and Ronald M. Brooks, *Come, Let Us Reason* (Grand Rapids, Mich.: Baker, 1990), 17.

6   George MacDonald, *The Curate's Awakening* (Minneapolis: Bethany, 1985), 161.

Study Guide

CHAPTER ONE: THE WISDOM OF CHANGE

1   Discuss the story told by Ravi Zacharias in this chapter of the thief searching for the jewels. How does this Eastern parable relate to America and the West today? What would you say is the primary pursuit of Western culture at this time?

2   Discuss the sense that something is missing spiritually in Western culture. What happens to a society when "the destiny of the soul is traded for the enthrallment of the moment"?

3   Is our modern cultural state new in the world's experience? What does the Bible have to say about it, particularly as it relates to the events in the book of Haggai?

4   Discuss how the radical student movements of the sixties have influenced America. What is your reaction to Ravi Zacharias' comment that "it is no longer the students rebelling against the system, it is the system itself that is in revolt against the very ideas on which it was built." What evidence for this statement can you find?

5   What are the differences between reason and intellect, the mind versus the brain? Discuss what makes up the "wholeness" of human beings and why education alone is not enough.

CHAPTER TWO: DYING BELIEFS AND STILLBORN HOPES

1 Discuss the confounding moral options we face today, where convictions may clash with "career goals," and religious belief clash with a "preferred lifestyle."

2 How are the foundations of our culture shifting? What may be the consequences of a major shift of this type? Why do you think more people don't see these shifts or raise an alarm?

3 Discuss secularization and the secular worldview that propels Western culture today. How is this "the first step on the road to unmanageable evil"?

4 Discuss the "philosophical attack upon the moorings of contemporary society." What is society's view of those who speak from a Christian perspective? What is its attitude toward religious ideas in general?

CHAPTER THREE: THE HIGH NOON OF PROMISE

1 What was America "created" for? What does the late scholar Russell Kirk, in his book *The Roots of American Order*, say our destiny will be?

2 Discuss pragmatism and the story of the train that laid its own track. How does this fit in with dreams of Utopia and narcissistic self-worship?

3 What four cities or cultures does Russell Kirk say have helped shape the American mind? Discuss what each has contributed to our cultural legacy.

4 Discuss the ancient Greek culture and its influence on this nation. What does Dr. Kirk say killed that great nation? According to Alexis de Tocqueville, what was the most important force holding America together?

5 Discuss the idea of "relativism" in ancient Greek and modern American culture. What belief did America once have which it now rejects?

CHAPTER FOUR: THE STORMS OF CONFLICT

1 Discuss the origins of the shift away from Christianity and toward secularization in Western culture. What conditions does Canadian historian David Marshall list as making a country inhospitable to the Christian message? Where does he place most of the blame?

2 What does Peter Berger say about the role of Protestants in the movement toward secularization? How did the "higher" or "historical" criticism damage scriptural authority? Do you believe this has had a damaging impact on American culture?

3 Discuss the paragraph on the Church of the Holy Sepulcher in Jerusalem. In what way is this a parable of Western Christianity today?

4 How has the secular view of the supernatural influenced Christian beliefs? Discuss how—in the name of "progress" and "sensitivity to other thought systems"—the Christian believer has been bullied and intimidated.

5 Discuss recent translations of the Bible, as in the example on page 52. Do you think politically correct versions help or hurt the cause of Christ? Do they help or hinder the American mission of reconciling liberty and law?

CHAPTER FIVE: THE TWILIGHT OF DECENCY

1 If secularization throws out God as the "irrational supernatural," what is man's point of reference? How does this redefine the role of conscience? How is the Christian voice being treated in the new world of secularism?

2   How do secularists defend their choices? What is their first principle? Discuss some of the tricks and strategies employed by those with a strictly secular world-view.

3   Discuss C. S. Lewis' thoughts from *The Pilgrim's Regress*. What insights does Lewis have to offer about the Spirit of the Age?

4   What does a loss of shame in a society do to a civilization? How does shame act as a guardian for ourselves and others? And how does a lack of shame lead to great evil?

5   Discuss the origins of secularism, according to the book of Genesis. What has secularization given us?

CHAPTER SIX: WITH DEFERENCE FOR DIFFERENCE

1   Discuss pluralism, multiculturalism, and ethnocentrism. What is the difference between self-acceptance and self-exaltation?

2   Discuss how the sixties radicals changed Western thinking. What did the "new America" believe? What became the "in thing" and the outrageous thing? How did the Indian scholar, Vivekananda, prefigure these changes in 1893?

3   Discuss the reshaping elements of pluralism and their dangers. How have the huge numbers of new immigrants changed our country? What are the implications when many citizens here speak a foreign language?

4   Discuss the drastic shift in American religious commitment from a predominantly Protestant society to a new influx of Catholic, and recently Islamic, Buddhist, Hindu, and New Age teachings. What is the strength of pluralism, and what is its great hazard?

5   What is the difference between opinion and conviction? How does love figure into this? Discuss the passage in this chapter by Malcolm Muggeridge.

CHAPTER SEVEN: THE FLICKERING FLAME OF REASON

1 "The assumption that all ideas are equally true is false." Why is one idea chosen over another? What is a symptom of a society that has lost its ability to think critically?

2 Discuss the book *Bridge on the River Kwai* by Pierre Boulle, regarding losing sight of the big picture by warring over lesser principles. How do pluralism, diversity, and freedom figure into this?

3 Discuss the meaning of "culture." What is the massive barrier that pluralism brings? Cultures operate in ways that are fundamentally opposed to each other. How do the stories of the Indian movies and the UCLA murder illustrate cultural differences?

4 Name and discuss Paul Tillich's three kinds of cultures as they relate to religious knowledge. Can our culture absorb all these and still remain autonomous? What costly doctrine does pluralism breed? Discuss examples of this in American today.

5 What is "the law of either/or"? What does the eradication of difference signal? Comment on Shakespeare (see page 100). Discuss Richard Weaver's statement on feelings. How have we, in America, elevated feelings above all?

CHAPTER EIGHT: THE DISORIENTED SELF

1 What may be the most astonishing reversal of the twentieth century? Discuss privatization of religion. What has this done to Christianity in the West? What has it done to public life?

2 How have secularization, pluralization, and privatization affected society? List two reasons why we know privatization is a false premise. Discuss how President Lincoln became the man he was. Can public and private behavior be severed?

3 Why is there no coherence in our communities? Discuss Arthur Miller's play *The Death of a Salesman* in this context.

4 Discuss how the trial of O. J. Simpson encapsulates the three-fold evils with which we now live. How does evil come to us through ideas?

5 Discuss the failures that felled the Graeco-Roman world. Do you see these aspects in Western culture today?

CHAPTER NINE: ESTABLISHING BOUNDARIES

1 What are some of the ways that God speaks to us? How does He speak to us through the arena of history?

2 Discuss God's love for His creation. What do you think of G. K. Chesterton's remark concerning this?

3 Read and discuss Shelley's poem "Ozymandias." What does this tell us about the importance of people and things in our world?

4 The time period of the seventh century before Christ had radical swings in the nation of Judah when it was led by the destructive king, Manasseh. What potent reminder does this history lesson have for us today?

CHAPTER TEN: PULLING DOWN THE FENCES

1 King Manasseh found it easier to destroy a nation than to re-build it. He made three decisions that altered Judah's course and led her to a tragic fate. What was the first and most radical choice he made?

2 What do the Scriptures say Manasseh did that provoked the Lord to anger? Why do you think he wanted to take down all the barriers his father and God had put up? Why do people want to do so today? What are the results?

3 Discuss the Peggy Noonan article in this chapter. People celebrate when each old rule is broken. Are we a better or happier society today with our modern "no rules" world?

4 When any belief is expelled, it will be replaced by another. What is the second step Manasseh took? What heinous practice did this lead to? Do we do anything similar today?

5 What is the third and final step Manasseh took? What could he have learned about this action if he had studied history beforehand?

6 Discuss the three profound lessons we can learn from Manasseh's life. What is the greatest lesson? Can people change dramatically? Discuss Manasseh's changed life and that of the Australian lady.

CHAPTER ELEVEN: RESTORING THE SOUL

1 The problem of evil seems so overwhelming that people don't know how to confront it. What should be their first step?

2 Nations can return to good. What historically proven steps did Josiah take to restore the nation of Judah? Discuss Daniel Webster's comment on a nation without God.

3 What was the treasure that Josiah gave back to his people? What is the greatest contribution of the Hebrews to the young American nation?

4 Discuss the importance of worship in maintaining the nation's moral strength. Why is reverence at the heart of worship? Discuss the word "sacred" and its opposite "profane." How has the soul of a nation changed?

5 What are several important consequences that follow Josiah's two simple steps? What peace did Josiah offer his people? What peace did the airmen in Vietnam find in the hymn? (See Isaiah 26:3.)

6   Read and discuss the Malcolm Muggeridge piece in this chapter. Does it remind you of Shelley's poem in chapter nine? What is the answer that Muggeridge presents?

CHAPTER TWELVE: THE UNMASKING OF EVIL

1   Discuss the mindless evil acts that seem to occur constantly in America. Are things getting worse? What is your reaction to the author's statement, "Evil is in the self-absorbed human heart"?

2   What are the three steps in unraveling the mystery of wickedness? How are words redefined to justify acts of evil, as in the example from the movie "Pulp Fiction"? What does God say about this kind of overt redefinition of language?

3   What are the components of wickedness? How can it be defined? Discuss C. S. Lewis' book, *The Abolition of Man*. How does the author's encounter with the man in Hong Kong parallel Lewis' book?

4   Discuss the thoughts of Dietrich Bonhoffer as he goes to his death for his stand against Hitler? Who will answer his call for responsible people who answer the call of God?

CHAPTER THIRTEEN: THE GOD WHO IS NEAR

1   God is not calling on us just to act more civilly. What does He want of us?

2   What was the instrument Jesus used to counter evil in the wilderness? What did Peter say of "religious experiences"?

3   Read and discuss the experience of Hien Pham in the Vietnamese communist prison. Is there any place too far removed for God to reach? Discuss also William Cowper's poem from this chapter.

4 What is the invitation to America and all the world? Discuss some hopeful signs that God is still transforming lives and souls, even in the midst of great evil.

About the Author

RAVI ZACHARIAS, president of Atlanta-based Ravi Zacharias International Ministries, was born in India. He immigrated to Canada in 1966 and studied at Trinity Evangelical Divinity School in Deerfield, Illinois, and Cambridge University in England. The author of *A Shattered Visage: The Real Face of Atheism, Cries of the Heart,* and *Can Man Live Without God,* he has addressed the issue of God's existence in many university settings including Harvard and Princeton in the U.S., as well as several prominent universities around the world. He has lectured in more than fifty countries, and his weekly radio program, "Let My People Think," is broadcast on more than 550 stations around the world. He and his wife, Margie, are the parents of three children, Sarah, Naomi, and Nathan.

The Ravi Zacharias International Ministries internet web sit is
http://www.rzim.com

In the tradition of C.S. Lewis and Francis Schaeffer comes one of this decade's most compelling works.

CAN MAN LIVE WITHOUT GOD

RAVI ZACHARIAS

WORD PUBLISHING

Available in book and audio formats at bookstores everywhere.